"Isn't it wise, especially in a cultural crisis, to pay attention to the poets and the prophets? Poet Adrienne Rich asks us to ponder two questions: 'With whom do you cast your lot,' and 'from whence does your energy come?' Prophetic theologian and justice-seeker John Snow asks us to tell the truth incarnationally because it truly matters where we place our bodies, with whom we pledge our love and loyalty, and how passionately we embrace the spiritual calling to create together, always together, a 'new heaven and earth.' Kudos to editor Rick Stecker for bringing this volume to print because, God knows Snow's kind of savvy cultural critique and compassionate wisdom is welcome sustenance for the journey."

—Marvin M. Ellison
Willard S. Bass Professor Emeritus of Christian Ethics, Bangor
Theological Seminary; Director of Alumni/ae Relations,
Union Theological Seminary

"Snow's work represents a thoughtful, provocative, and problematic reflection on a basic American, and probably human, paradox: We must compete with others while also taking care of them. Conflict exists side-by-side with cooperation; rivalry with love; and hierarchy with a sense of equality. Snow approaches these tensions from the perspective of a liberal Episcopal priest, and while his insights are perhaps most applicable to the privileged Christian communities of which he was a part, they will be relevant to a wide variety of contemporary readers."

—Craig Greenman
Associate Professor of Philosophy, Colby-Sawyer College

"John Snow critically explores the Enlightenment roots of our tyrannical obsession with the individual self. He points to the exuberant liberation made possible by faith in Jesus, the Word-made-flesh, to redefine human community and the full life as God desires for us all. Frederick Stecker's braiding of excerpts of John Snow's sermons are themselves bright, succinct 'incarnations' by which we encounter Snow's revelations of God's hope for us. This book belongs in every preacher's study."

—A. Robert Hirschfeld
Bishop of the Episcopal Church of New Hampshire

"If there is anyone left out there who really cares to discover the roots of the deep trouble in which we find ourselves these days, both as a culture and as a Christian community, this book is serious help of the first order. John Snow was a brilliant mind and a loving soul whose clear voice it is wonderful to hear again."

—Thom Blair, Jr.

"John Snow's sharp analysis of achievement and class is a profound moment in human relationships. It belongs in the hearts and on the tongues of everyone—politician, voter, educator, student, preacher, and parishioner—who would do justice, love mercy, and walk humbly upon the earth."

—John L. Hooker
Sometime Professor of Liturgy, Homiletics, and Music,
Episcopal Divinity School

"John Snow had the compassionate heart of a pastor, the keen mind of a theologian, and the mischievous wit of a social commentator. His gift for articulating deep truths makes this previously unpublished work every bit as current as when it was first penned. Just when our collective fear of 'losing' threatens to overtake the principles we claim, John Snow calls us to find our better selves, individual and societal."

—Alan M. Gates
Episcopal Bishop of Massachusetts

"With the keen eye of a prophet, John Snow lays bare the hidden worldview that pervades American society and shapes every aspect of our lives. Social Darwinism is in the air we breathe and the water we drink. From marriage to education, politics to sports, medicine to ministry, we are ruled by patterns of competition that divide the world into 'winners' and 'losers.' In provocative, sometimes searing, chapters that interweave essays and sermons, Snow unmasks the fear of death that drives our aggression, and he lifts up an alternative Christian vision: a community set free to live with compassion, justice, and mercy. Snow's powerful insights are even more relevant today than when they were first expressed, and we can be grateful to Rick Stecker for presenting them to new readers with such powerful effect. This is a bracing and inspiring book."

—Margaret Bullitt-Jonas
Missioner for Creation Care, Episcopal Diocese of Western Massachusetts

I Win, We Lose

John H. Snow (1924–2008), Professor of Pastoral Theology, Episcopal Divinity School (1972–1990).

I Win, We Lose

The New Social Darwinism and the Death of Love

— And Other Writings —

For Bob Gainer

JOHN HALL SNOW

Edited by
FREDERICK STECKER

Foreword by
HARVEY H. GUTHRIE

Watermelon, Watermelon & Blessings

Boy Stecker

WIPF & STOCK · Eugene, Oregon

August 7, 2016

I WIN, WE LOSE
The New Social Darwinism and the Death of Love
And Other Writings

Wipf & Stock
An Imprint of Wipf and Stock Publishers
199 W. 8th Ave., Suite 3
Eugene, OR 97401

www.wipfandstock.com

ISBN 13: 978-1-4982-0062-2

Manufactured in the U.S.A.   01/11/2016

In Memory of Other Prophets:
Jonathan N. Mitchell
Robert DeWitt
Lyman Cunningham Ogilby

Contents

Foreword

In 1962 John Snow joined the clergy staff of Christ Church, Harvard Square, Cambridge, MA, where my family worshipped on Sundays. He was one of the best preachers I had ever heard. On the one hand, he spoke in a kind of unpolished, straightforward, no-nonsense, almost naïve way. On the other hand, his sermons were sophisticated expositions of the Biblical texts and eye-opening reflections on literature, culture, human nature, and the social context in which we were worshipping. There were no histrionics, no pretentious professional polish: it was the depth and power of the content that took hold of me. As a friend of mine was wont to say of sermons that really got to him, John's preaching "lifted my load."

Ten years later, in 1972, I traveled to Princeton—where, since 1968, he had been the Episcopal Church's campus minister—to ask John Snow to join the faculty of the Episcopal Theological School as professor of pastoral theology. It was one of the best things I ever did as dean there.

In the curriculum of a seminary, "pastoral theology" is a "how-to" discipline. It can become simply that, dealing only with practice and technique, leaving "theology" to the more theoretical parts of the curriculum. Of course, adequate preparation for ministry must involve the development of expertise in the actual practice of ministry: priests must be schooled in how to function as priests. But ministerial practice divorced from, and/or devoid of, understanding of the faith that gives rise to the practice, as well as understanding of the cultural setting and presuppositions in which the practice takes place, is lacking in both effectiveness and integrity.

Donald Schon, professor of urban studies and education at the Massachusetts Institute of Technology in those days, coined the term "reflective practitioner" to describe the kind of person he believed graduate professional education—in law schools and medical schools and business schools and so on—should produce.[1] He held that the best professionals are those in whom theory and practice, technique and interpretation, go on inseparably. This usually unarticulated, largely unexamined process involves, as Schon put it, "reflection-in-action," and he saw the goal of professional schools as fostering this vital creativity in future professionals.

Schon contributed a great deal to my understanding of what should be the goal of education for ministry in theological seminaries. More to the point in what I am writing here, he articulated what I sensed and admired in John Snow. John was himself a reflective practitioner par excellence. That is what I had seen in him at Christ Church, and that is what led to my courting him on that trip to Princeton. I was so thankful that, after characteristically raising penetrating questions about himself and theological seminaries, he decided to join us. Whatever theoretical terms he himself might have used, his goal as professor of pastoral theology was to develop reflective practitioners. He would be the first, with characteristic honesty, to say that not all of them "got it." Those who did are, like me, very grateful.

To his life as reflective practitioner he brought a thorough education in literature embodying the mood and presuppositions and understanding of human nature present in the culture in which he lived, having done his undergraduate work at Harvard and a master's degree in American literature at Columbia. What he learned as student was honed and deepened as he taught several years in elementary school, becoming headmaster of St. Michael's Country Day School in Newport, RI, from 1951 to 1955.

At that time, St. Michael's was associated with Trinity Episcopal Church in Newport. It was there that, as his obituary in *The*

1. Schon, *The Reflective Practitioner.*

Shelburne Falls Independent put it, "He became a Christian and decided to study for the ministry." Reflective practitioner that he already was as teacher and headmaster, he apparently came to see Christian commitment and theological perspective as necessary elements in the practice and reflection to which he was called. He graduated from the Episcopal Theological School and was ordained in 1958, serving as an assistant at Christ Episcopal Church in Hamilton, MA, and then as director of Gould Farm, a residential mental health community, before joining the staff of Christ Church, Cambridge, in 1962. Thus, his experience as a priest of the Episcopal Church involved the pastoral care of people in parishes as well as involvement in a therapeutic community.

Individuals do not exist in vacuums. Pastoral ministry takes place in specific historical and cultural settings. Significant elements in the historical context of John's reflective practice of pastoral ministry in the sixties were the Civil Rights Movement and the Vietnam War.

His role at Christ Church in that context was significant. The people of that parish not only participated in civil rights demonstrations and marches; Christ Church was one of the few church bodies that turned a significant part of its endowed resources over to African American institutions as reparation for the sin of slavery. Christ Church was also a center of resistance to the war in Vietnam. John, who had served in as a rigger and then as a medic during World War II, but who opposed our involvement in Vietnam, was instrumental in bringing Dr. Martin Luther King, Jr. and Dr. Benjamin Spock to Christ Church for a nationally viewed press conference opposing the role the United States was playing in Vietnam. For John, social issues, peace and justice issues, as well as personal crises and illnesses, were pastoral issues.

His critique of contemporary ministry in the church and his understanding of what ministry should involve were recently characterized in this way: "John Snow said that mainline Christianity mostly seeks management/therapist type clergy, who are ill equipped to shepherd the church through the rough shoals of a post-Christian society."[2]

For John, the equipment required for ministry includes an understanding of human history as *corporate* rather than individual and as *taking place in the presence of the God* of the classic Biblical prophets and Jesus Christ. Precisely pastoral ministry—the healing and support of a church and church members negotiating "the rough shoals of a post-Christian society"—must be grounded in an understanding of the forces at work in the human community in light of the just and loving purposes of God.

John Snow's reflection on the world in which the church ministers today led to his conviction that the force driving the human enterprise in his place and time, in both its social and individual aspects, is Social Darwinism, the extension of Charles Darwin's epochal understanding of biological history as an ongoing struggle in which, by a process he called natural selection, some forms of life survived while others did not into the areas of the human mind and of society and culture. Our lot is cast in an all-inclusive process in which those forms of life somehow fitting nature's ways survive, while those lacking fall by the wayside. Social Darwinism understands "fitness" in an evaluative sense: those who are fit, as opposed to those who are unfit, win in the struggle for survival.

John's *I Win, We Lose: The New Social Darwinism and the Death of Love* is the result of a lifetime of study and reflection, teaching and pastoral ministry with people. It describes the effects of Social Darwinism in the areas of marriage, racial relations, education, social and religious institutions, and the contingency of life. John saw Social Darwinism as a pervasive disease infecting contemporary social and political and economic life, as spawning and then driving a culture obsessed with winning. It underlay the imperialistic presumptuousness that has come to be called "American exceptionalism." It justified unbridled, laissez-faire capitalism that is leaving 99 percent of the world's wealth in the hands of 1 percent of its population. Embraced as an ideology by even those

2. The Rev. Bill Blaine-Wallace in a January 26, 2014 sermon at All Saints Episcopal Church, Skowhegan, ME.

not really winners in a Social Darwinist culture, it became an instrument of their own oppression.

The consequence of that in John's understanding of God and the Christian life was a rejection of seeing Christ's death as substitutionary atonement for "my" sins. I heard him say more than once that St. Anselm's doctrine of the atonement, as restitution for our sins, is the source of the fundamental neurosis of Western society. The problem for John is a corporate problem, a demonic possession of the human community and enterprise by Social Darwinism's win / lose / survival understanding of life.

But if it is not a matter of "my" being saved by the sacrificial death of Christ, neither is it a matter of some Social Darwinist struggle with the demons. John wrote, "What we are placed here by God to do as Jesus came here to do, is not to root out and destroy the evil and darkness and cruelty in the world or in our own hearts, it is to let it be redeemed by love." And for him we let it do that as we live the life of Jesus in the community of Jesus' followers, in the church, serving others and witnessing to God's love for all. He wrote:

> The Christian community must become, like the early church, an alternative community where survival is recognized as entirely within the purview of a loving God, and the business of Christians becomes mutual care and concern in an atmosphere of prayerful attention as they serve each other and the world. Love is manifested in the corporate life of the church in Christ, and regularly rehearsed in the sacramental celebration of the Eucharist. Christian morality takes place in the context of repentance, forgiveness, service and compassion.

Lacking in John's writings is any systematic doctrinal discussion of God or Jesus or the church. Just as his concern with Social Darwinism is not with it as theory, but about its consequences in our culture, our life, so his understanding of Christianity is not theoretical or doctrinal but in terms of life lived in the Christian community, with living together with Jesus in God's love. I love

this reminiscence by Donald Schell, a founder of the Church of St. Gregory of Nyssa (1980) in San Francisco:

> I phoned John Snow, the Episcopal chaplain at Princeton, my pastor, and one of the best preachers I'd ever heard (or have heard since). "John, I need to talk to you. I think I'm becoming an Episcopalian." John and I had a great conversation. I told him all the theological stuff I was working on and he said, "We've got plenty of room for you." I told him I thought the Episcopal Church was actually a mess theologically, a church without a backbone, incapable of standing for anything. He predicted that I would come to appreciate that—and so I have.

The point is that, for John, "theological stuff," theory and doctrine, were not primary. In his words, "Love is manifested in the corporate life of the church in Christ, and regularly rehearsed in the sacramental celebration of the Eucharist. Christian morality takes place in the context of repentance, forgiveness, service and compassion."

But he was no anti-intellectual. He arrived there by way of rigorous, disciplined, thoughtful study and reflection on things historical and cultural, on human institutions and relationships. He was a reflective practitioner in the Anglican tradition of learned parsons. He anticipated what is now called "weak theology" as, in contrast to Social Darwinism's winner / loser / survival struggle, he pointed us toward a powerless love that will graciously outlast every power. I am most grateful for the light he has shed on the human condition in our time and place, and on what it is to seek to follow Jesus in our time and place.

And I am grateful to Frederick Stecker for the researching and editing involved in this collection of John's writings. I am honored to be asked by him and by Mary Snow to pay this tribute to a prophetic priest and a good man.

Harvey H. Guthrie
Dean Emeritus
Episcopal Divinity School

Preface

There is a story that circulates among the clergy who knew John Snow recalling a time when, early in his appointment at The Episcopal Theological School, the secretary of Christ Church, Cambridge, called him at his office. An individual wanted to make his confession and had asked to see John in particular. John relented and walked around the corner to the offices at Christ Church. The individual asked to be absolved for his many sins. As he unloaded his life's concerns in some detail and for some time, the man concluded by asking again for absolution. John Snow replied, "I am a priest and I will grant you the absolution you have requested, but I want you to know that as an individual you've told me the details of the most wasted and self-centered life I've ever heard, and if I were a lay person, I wouldn't have a thing to do with you." Snow granted absolution, and the two parted company.

Several years later, Snow was at a gathering at a hotel and was approached by a person saying, "I'm sure you don't remember me but I am the one who asked for your absolution several years ago and I wanted to thank you. I have turned my life completely around." Surprised, Snow asked, "What do you mean?" The man replied that he had been to counselors, psychiatrists, A.A., social workers, as well as to his doctor, and no one had been able to help him. "Go on," said Snow. The man said, "You were the only one who could tell me the truth."

The Rev. John Snow, a professor of pastoral theology at the Episcopal Divinity School (1972–1990), knew *how* to tell the truth.

Jim Chapman

In the capacity of pastoral theologian, he was one who paid close attention to the cultural context in which theology takes place. He stepped back from social movements to ask "why is this happening and where can we find God in this?" Then he urged us to look in that direction. He was also a student of the societal influences that made ministry succeed or fail. John Snow has had many followers asking him to untangle what was happening in the church, in ministry, in marriage, in government, in society, and, like the man who asked for absolution, in their personal lives.

I am one of those followers. In 1985, I was a Procter Fellow in Religion and Psychology at the Episcopal Divinity School in Cambridge, MA, and had the honor of having John as my tutor. In my preliminary interview to set up a focus of study, my initial question to him was, "Why is it that in worship I can move my hands upward and the whole congregation stands or move them downwards and everyone sits; yet in a meeting with the church board, the same kind of control is non-existent and the meetings seem to have nothing to do with what we should be doing as members of the Christian faith?" John replied, "I think you need to understand the psychoanalytic aspects of transference and dependence; start out by reading Janet Malcolm's *The Impossible Profession,* and we'll go on from there. Let's meet weekly for an hour or two and see where that leads us."

Thus began a sixteen-week study in which my readings ranged from psychoanalyst Leo Stone to leadership psychologist Manfred Kets de Vries, and from Sigmund Freud to Winifred Bion, Melanie Klein, and the object-relations school of psychoanalytic study. I began to understand the psychological aspects of religion as well as the dynamics of small and large groups. After my study with John, I kept in touch sending him occasional professional papers that I published as well as, near the time of his death, a partial draft of my book analyzing the use of stealth religious language in American political rhetoric.

Shortly after John's death, in 2008, I re-discovered a 136-page unedited and undated manuscript entitled *I Win, We Lose: The New Social Darwinism and the Death of Love* in my midden of research notes. I had acquired these papers around 1990 from an old friend, the Rev. John Crocker, who was another of Snow's followers. I had forgotten about the manuscript in the years that had passed. Upon reading the manuscript some eighteen years later, I knew that this work needed to be reintroduced to a new generation of Christians; the systemic issues were the same as those facing us these days. Snow's prophetic proclamation of justice and love needed to be heard once more. He was telling us something about ourselves and he was telling us the truth. I received permission from Mary Snow, John's widow, to edit these papers as well as to add insights from a collection of sermons from Christ Church, Cambridge, MA, where John was referred to as "Preacher-in-Residence."

Stitching snippets of sermons like patches onto the draft manuscript was not a simple matter. John was my mentor and I had to overcome my admiration of his mind and our friendship. Further, the events John described from the late sixties onward contrasted with my first-hand experience from a generation's difference. It was a time of personal, social, and institutional disorientation fed by the insane belief that everything of value could be reliably measured, quantified, and evaluated—including human beings. As I look back on my own life, it is very valuable to have Snow's perspective.

This book, therefore, is composed of written materials from several sources that stretch over a period of twenty-five years; his work is in the neighborhood of thirty to forty years old. As the Episcopal Chaplain at Princeton, Snow began observing political, economic, and social upheavals and began to ponder the origins of America's dis-ease; in his years at the Episcopal Divinity School he began to compile these observations into five books and the paper I rediscovered. What troubled Snow back then continues to haunt us today.

Back then: one has only to compare the post-Korean War America with the political and social culture of the late sixties and the early seventies.[1] While our country was transfixed by the Cold

---

1. I advance similar comparisons in Stecker, *The Podium, the Pulpit and the Republicans: How Presidential Candidates Use Religious Language in American*

War in the fifties and early sixties, life at home was predictable and comfortable. Being an American meant sticking to a rigid system of behavior and beliefs. Communities were local entities: not only did we know the minister, the doctor, and the pharmacist by name, but we also knew the mailman, the mechanic, and the grocer. We had a shared sense of story with them, and everyone had, it seemed, an assigned place in life. For most of white America, life resembled a more or less sophisticated version of the TV sitcom, *The Adventures of Ozzie and Harriet.*

Within a decade all of that had changed. Conformity, the glue that held us together and defined us in post-World War II America, was no longer an adhesive. While American troops were fighting in Vietnam, other wars were being fought at home. An overview of some of the events of 1969 tells the story. The US government secretly bombed Cambodia. The Chicago Seven were tried for creating riots at the Democratic National Convention in 1968. A three-day rock concert took place in Bethel, New York; it became known as "Woodstock" and changed popular culture forever. In New York City, there were riots protesting the harassment of homosexuals at the Stonewall Café. Black students at Cornell University took over Willard Straight Hall and demanded a Black Studies program. At Harvard, 300 members of the Students for a Democratic Society seized an administration building, an occupation that resulted in 184 arrests and injured 48 persons. General Electric endured a winter-long strike by its employees; it was followed by a postal workers' strike and a walkout of 500,000 at General Motors. Further, Cleveland's Cuyahoga River caught fire from industrial pollutants, and the Buffalo River, New York, was monitored for the same threat.

Back then Snow began to tell us what he believed was happening to us and to our country. Just as the demons rebuked Jesus when confronted with Truth, so too, Snow suggests, the pain of the rigid class system was working itself out by the rejection (or at least the questioning) of everything and everyone that represented the establishment. Dick and Jane were no longer characteristic of

---

Political Debate, 11–12.

children in the American family. *I Win, We Lose: The New Social Darwinism and the Death of Love* was composed in rough draft. As the editor of this project, it is my hope that John Snow will be teaching us once more.

Why is his perspective relevant to today's Christian seeking to understand the role of the church? Because, in John's words,

> What becomes apparent is that those who have made the choice to attend church expect, or even demand, that it will speak to their sense of disorientation in time and space, and to their deep anxiety in the midst of the ever changing and unpredictable. People attend church looking for historical and generational continuity and, beyond that, ultimate safety. They want to belong in history; the safety they seek is not biological. They want the assurance of their worth.[2]

The first chapter is devoted to Social Darwinism's popularity in America. Snow outlines the mutation of Darwin's evolutionary theories to fit into Herbert Spencer's social theory, now dubbed Social Darwinism. These origins are traced to the Enlightenment thinker, John Locke. Locke marked a transition between medieval thinking regarding the sanctity of labor and the divine right of kings to a new view of the Social Contract—one that was not imposed by the government but consented to by the governed. Locke believed in the right of an individual to own property based on natural rights and natural law. He also believed in only enough government to ensure that one's property was protected, but not so much as to interfere with individual freedom. Locke had no use for the unfortunate. Locke's ideas, paired with Spencer's Social Darwinist theories, provided the ideological fertile soil for westward expansion of America. The first chapter is an important theoretical platform for the rest of Snow's observations and it is, in my view, a daunting read. Yet today we witness this same contest of ideologies concerning the common good. It is found in the question of whether conservative and libertarian *individualism* (with as little as possible interference from government) in Republican and Tea

2. Personal correspondence, dated April 22, 1986.

Party movements, is more important for the preservation of our Republic than the values of liberal Democrats and the progressives trusting in government and espousing *collaboration*. If one becomes mired in this chapter's complexity, the reader is encouraged to go on to the following chapters and return to it at a later time.

Especially significant to me are Snow's descriptions of the social shifts that occurred in the post-World War II and Korean War era that are detailed in the ensuing chapters of this book. I chortled through John's comparison of the older riggers' philosophical discussions at the Navy yard as contrasted with attitudes of certainty found in young college graduates. The satellite Sputnik created a space race and an emphasis on standardized testing to measure one's abilities and acceptability for a higher education. The G.I. Bill of Rights gave working-class individuals the opportunity to enter college and created a shift not only in class but also in community (chapter 2). Snow's personal friendship with Martin Luther King as well as his involvement in the Civil Rights Movement enabled him to describe the theological commitments that led to King's public opposition to the Vietnam War that cost King his life (chapter 3). Snow ponders King's achievements and questions their lasting effect in a society that continues to pit individuals (young and old, male and female, black and white) against each other.

What constituted family changed with the growth of suburbia as well as the advent of the birth control pill. Snow applies Bateson's theory of complementary and symmetrical relations between nations to the institution of marriage and its instability (chapter 4). In chapter 5, Snow studies the meta-communication or the messaging of institutions and the media to meet societal aspirations of its consumers. Snow reminisces on an experiment in theological education regarding the mergers of two seminaries where their attempt at educational reform instead was met by resistance from the larger church.

Chapter 6 examines the limits that define a society and the challenge to those limits by the social influences of American individualism. Since winning is meaningless without the concept of losing, he argues, then our continuing the destructive capacities of the new Social Darwinism are not only legion, but now irrevers-ible. The desire to win pushes other human beings to the margins and, as it does, it ignores environmental and social consequenc-es—sealing our own fate.

In his concluding chapter, Snow observes that Darwin never applied his theory to a single species and challenges the assump-tions of Social Darwinism and its byproducts. Snow urges us to make our corporate life more just and loving. Snow asks us to un-derstand the planet Earth as a part of a created order, and that it, too, has a definitive and limited lifespan. This made me realize just how much "survival" unintentionally remains a part of my psycho-logical make-up and verbal lexicon. We have a great deal to gain by resurrecting the observations of this important theologian; we also have so much to refigure and relearn.

My goal in editing this work is to immerse the reader in the broader scope of John Snow's theological perspective by lacing to-gether illustrations taken from sermons that augment his observa-tions; these sermon snippets, framed here by a wider margin and a set of horizontal lines, were not a part of the original manuscript. Since Snow believed that the meaning of human life is not at all obvious, it is my desire that this book will enhance our conversa-tion about life's purpose.

Acknowledgments

I am grateful to those who have helped me along the way. I owe personal thanks to copy editors and friends Kate Seamans, Ela Kotkowska, and Jane Redmont for untangling my prose as well as for having an understanding of stylistic manuals required to complete this task. The Rev. Gordon Dean was present at the initial meetings with Mary Snow to conceive of this work and has been a constant source of encouragement. For the better part of a year Louise Ambler, archivist of Christ Church, Cambridge, sorted through church files to photocopy sermons preached by John Snow while assistant and then preacher-in-residence of her parish. Hers was truly a labor of love for the Snow family doubly fueled by her investment to bring John's theological legacy back to the public attention. Of course, I express my deep appreciation to Mary Snow and her son Tom for giving me guidance in the shaping of this work as well as permission to take on this task. Friends Thom Blair and John Hooker gave the book final readings, while my wife, Ann Page Stecker, provided constant support seasoned with a healthy critique of my work. The last quote of the book, "At the baptism of Jesus," appeared both in sermon form from the archives of Christ Church, Cambridge, as well as in print in Snow's book *A Vocation to Risk*. It is reprinted by permission of Cowley Press. Finally, I wish to thank the editors at Wipf & Stock Press for seeing the value in Snow's work as well as affirming my desire to make the publication costs accessible to the general reader.

Frederick Stecker
The Season of Epiphany, 2016

Abbreviations

DDT	dichlorodiphenyltrichloroethane, an insecticide
DNA	deoxyribonucleic acid
FBI	Federal Bureau of Investigation
GI Bill (of Rights)	The Servicemen's Readjustment Act of 1944, PL 78–346, 58 Stat. 284m
GOE	General Ordination Examination
GRE	Graduate Record Examination
IQ	intelligence quotient
LSAT	Law School Admission Test
NIH	National Institutes of Health
MIT	Massachusetts Institute of Technology
NAACP	National Association for the Advancement of Colored People
PSAT	Preliminary SAT
rDNA	recombinant DNA
SAT	Scholastic Aptitude Test
SCLC	Southern Christian Leadership Conference
SSAT	Secondary School Admission Test
UN	United Nations

1

Social Darwinism and Its Bequest

Winning and Losing as the Basis of America Culture

HOW SOCIAL DARWINISM FOUND FERTILE SOIL

Human beings are organized by memory and language. If there is such a thing as instinct, we have less of it than animals and insects. We do not know who we are until we have been told. We do not know what to do with our lives until a number of possibilities have been presented to us by language. Whatever is new, we improvise out of what we have been already told. Our genes have programmed us to listen, remember, and speak. Without our history, we are the most maladaptive of creatures. To the extent that we are social creatures, language and memory provide most of the order in our corporate life.

This being so, the fact that human behavior is less genetically determined made the reception the Western world gave to Charles Darwin's *The Origin of Species* (1859) a complete surprise. Watershed theories—whole quantum jumps of enlightenment—do not often have immediate popular effect, but within a decade of its appearance, Darwin's theory of evolution was being dealt with in newspaper editorials and cartoons, from the pulpit, in lecture halls, or wherever people gathered to talk. The first reaction was negative, generated and led by Christians, and had to do with Darwin's claim that humans evolved over the ages from lower forms of life. In the popular imagination this took the form of a simplistic statement: "Man was descended from the apes." More literal Christians argued passionately over the conflict between Darwin's theory and the Genesis story as regards the time span of creation, but the basic conflict had to do with the origin of humans. Were we quite a separate creation, made in God's image, given dominion over the Earth and all other creatures, or were we the slowly developed descendants of "lower" animals and hence, ourselves, irretrievably animal?

It seems a silly question today, since the evidence that we did, in fact, derive from lower forms of life has convinced most of us for almost a century and a half. All Christians but the most fundamentalist say that the Genesis story is important for its symbolic definition of what it is like to be human in relationship to God and the creation. All agree that it is not science or to be taken as scientific theory. The question, however, is not a silly one in its consequences.

The given nature of human corporate life is mutual service issuing in mutual trust. It is a small planet we live on. It is a creation as we are. It is limited in its resources, its capabilities, its space, its creativity, and even its life span. It was born, it thrives, and it may get sick and die an untimely death. What we call growth is what God calls greed, and what doctors call metastasis. It is a great sickness. We have been lording it over a world we should be serving. In wartime, if we accept the war, we accept service in sacrificial terms gladly, because these are clearly the terms of survival. Right now God is calling us to the reality of sacrificial mutual service for our sake, for each other's sake, and for the sake of the world.

From a sermon preached at Christ Church,
Cambridge, MA, November 11, 1973.

It is no surprise that those who first accepted Darwin's theory of human origins were those least appalled by it—those most affected by the Enlightenment (particularly by Locke and Rousseau) and who had, or seemed to have, a higher doctrine of human nature than either Protestantism or Catholicism. For them, one might say, anything was better than being the descendants of Adam and Eve. There was, as Whitman liked to point out, nothing sinful or depraved about animals. Those who resisted Darwin most passionately were not those who in the past had been merely concerned about the image of God in human beings, but those who had primarily emphasized the image of Adam, the "fallenness," the sinfulness, and the depravity of human nature. For these Christians, the whole point of Christ's intervention into history was to save humans from their sinful selves by His "blood atonement."

The church, for too long, seemed to be telling us that Jesus came to free us from our own rotten selves; that we have been rotten all along. What is it about being human that makes this view so prominent? We don't like to die; we don't like our mortality. We don't like to be sick or physically disabled. We don't like to be ugly; we don't like to be oppressed or limited in our choices. We don't like to grow old with a diminishment of physical power. But above all, what we dislike the most is the potential for unhappiness that persists throughout our lives, the sense of powerlessness that comes from suffering, or the idea of suffering. These we have taken as the givens, the non-negotiables of life.

This posture suggests that all these things that we don't like are not just one damn thing after another, but that there is a reason for them. [The eleventh-century theologian] Anselm made things worse by suggesting that we deserve them. Jesus then takes them upon himself in obedience to

God's will, as the doctrine goes. Technically, Jesus liberated us from this doctrine of sin, but not from guilt. If anything, it increased our guilt. While this doctrine was intended to make us feel grateful, it too often made us feel frightened and anxious. How can we trust that this God truly loves us, as sinful as we are? It makes sense out of sin but not out of salvation.

From a sermon preached at Christ Church,
Cambridge, MA, March 11, 1984.

Darwin's theory threw their whole salvational system into disequilibrium, at least at the level of the theology of creation. And yet there was another level at which Darwin's theory was a crushing confirmation of Calvinist Christianity. Calvin's doctrine of predestination, his teaching that God had arbitrarily chosen or elected certain individuals to be saved from the beginning of creation, was not unlike what philosopher and political theorist Herbert Spencer called Darwin's theory, "the survival of the fittest," a theory Spencer was to apply to matters social, political, and economic. As the "elect" were assumed by Calvin to be those individuals who were successful in business and chosen by God for salvation, so the "fittest" were those who won mating rights through challenge, and were chosen by natural selection for survival. Although Calvinists were, in theory, not to claim salvation for themselves but to accept by faith whatever God had decided, it seemed obvious to them that the elect were those who, by being chosen by God, prospered in their work. Spencer would not have disagreed. Both Calvin and Spencer, in practice, saw their belief in intelligent aggression (now applied to humans) as the mark of the saved and the survivor. This may, to some degree, explain why Spencer's application of Darwin's evolutionary theory to social thought so quickly dominated not only the intellectual world of the United States, but also those instrumental in settling the West—it fit them well.

The battle over creation was won hands down by the Darwinists in the scientific-intellectual arena, but it continued into the twenty-first century within the Christian community. There was, however, very little initial argument in the United States or Britain with Herbert Spencer's Social Darwinism. An evolutionary process within the human species guided by natural selection was too close to American distortions of the theology of Calvin, the economics of Adam Smith, the population theories of Malthus, and the cumulative experience of two countries leading the world in industrial expansion, to be effectively argued against. The United States was a country of such vast spaces and startling abundance that it seemed able to afford such a wasteful theory. It is also apparent that Social Darwinism provided a justification of sorts for the devastation of the Native American and the segregation of the recently freed American black. Most critically, it provided a modern, and even scientific, alternative to Calvin's doctrine of election that made it possible to accept poverty, unemployment, and misfortune generally, not so much a part of the human condition as preordained, but as a necessary part of progress, as contributing to the ultimate perfection of the human species.

Again, the millenarian nature of Social Darwinism, its promised ideal, made it attractive to people who had in the past liked to think of themselves as building a New Jerusalem. But, as opposed to the realized eschatology of building a New Jerusalem, which required some mutual care and a true Calvinist concern for social justice, Social Darwinism placed the matter of ethics and social justice in the distant future. Through natural selection, the "ideal" individual would eventually build a perfectly ethical "ideal" society with mutual concern, care, and cooperation as its central values. But, for the time being, the poor must be left to starve, and the non-productive old and the chronically ill to die, with the scant assurance that their deaths would hasten the coming of such a society.

Obviously, such neglect of the poor and the chronically ill was not acceptable to Christians, or, for that matter, to anyone with the last vestiges of sanity. When criticized by church leaders on this, Spencer replied that private or individual charity was a good thing because it developed a higher degree of altruism in the survivor (Spencer believed, as did naturalist Jean Baptiste Lamarck, that acquired characteristics were inherited). Spencer's concern, he said, was that the government do nothing altruistic—no poor laws, no public health, etc. This disclaimer helped even Christians to accept Social Darwinism, as they had already accepted the separation of church and state and the concept of morality as personal and private rather than social.

Christianity is a terrible problem solver. It is neither a spiritual problem solver nor a social or psychological technique; it runs into little but frustration and despair when it sees itself in this light. The purpose of Christianity—and not merely Christianity—is to help human beings find meaning and purpose in life, given the inevitable suffering and conflict, and assuming that the ultimate threat to meaning is the given that we all must die.

From "The Fear of Death and the Need to Accumulate"
(Unpublished Lecture, Episcopal Divinity School,
Cambridge, MA, Fall 1971)

Not much is known about the actual process by which a society assimilates a new social theory, but it must be assumed that the test of assimilation would be to the extent to which the theory penetrates the basic institutions of the society until it becomes, simply, an assumption, and requires little explicit articulation. It would be difficult to find a moment in history when a new social theory met so quickly with massive intellectual public acceptance as Spencer's Social Darwinism, but the extent to which it penetrated the institutional life of American society and became truly assimilated cannot be estimated purely on the basis of intellectual acceptance. American society is subject to fads, and fads by definition are popularly accepted ideas that are not institutionally assimilated. The assimilated social theory of American institutions up to the time of Social Darwinism was a not too comfortable mixture of Rousseau and Locke.

The Protestant inheritance of the majority of Americans caused them to hedge on Rousseau's extravagant claims of the goodness of human nature when it came to the actual ordering of society, but Rousseau's noble savage seems always lurking in our institutional forest, reminding us at least of the negative importance of nurture over nature. Far more important was the social theory of John Locke.[1]

FROM LOCKE TO SPENCER

George Cabot Lodge, in his *The New American Ideology*, lists five components to Lockean ideology: individualism, property rights, competition, the limited state, and scientific specialization and fragmentation. Spencer's Social Darwinism confirmed Lockean ideology, and, Lodge comments:

> . . . distortions, modifications, and exceptions notwithstanding, this ideology has never been explicitly inspected, renovated, or replaced . . . [but] remains a pervasive and quasi-religious entity which must not be called into question. However distorted or eroded, it has remained unassailably the primary source of legitimacy for our institutions, whether economic, political, or social. And this is so even though our most powerful institutions, large corporations in particular, have in fact departed substantially from it. Its resilience is formidable.[2]

One suspects that the most important assumptions about the nature of reality that any society holds are inevitably the least examined until the anomalies caused by the inadequacies of these assumptions become too painful for a society to bear. This movement was realized in America with the beginning of the Civil War, when the conflict between Locke's most basic values—individualism and the right to private property—plunged the nation into

1. In a section entitled "Freedom's Philosopher," Eduardo Galeano calls our attention to the fact that, while writing *An Essay Concerning Human Understanding*, Locke invested his savings in Royal African Stock. "That firm, owned by the British Crown and by 'the industrious and rational,' hunted and captured slaves in Africa and sold them in America." Galeano, *Mirrors*, 158.—Ed.

2. Lodge, *The New American Ideology*, 11.

bloody chaos. The question loomed, "Is there some point at which, a human individual, may become property?" Locke had, in his own writing, moved in that direction by declaring that an individual could sell his labor to another individual, at which point this labor became the property of the person who bought it. In the matter of slavery, then, the Lockean ideology, which had skirted the issue of full humanity of other races, broke down precisely because of the paradox built into its doctrine of human nature that defined human beings in terms of what they observably do, rather than in terms of origin. They are competitive, they own property, they specialize, etc. Locke had brought a clumsy empiricism to bear on the human situation that was to persist, particularly in America, and to become less clumsy.

Yet Locke, with other great figures of the Enlightenment, still claimed, if in a ritual sort of way, that each person had an inviolable soul given to him by God. Most Americans, although with varying conviction, believed this, too, as much in the South as in the North. Locke's idea of human perfectibility was met by claiming that the blacks could be property because they were less than human; no more, in fact, than horses or oxen or dogs.[3] The Southern religious establishment, almost without exception, accepted this argument.

It is fascinating to read Frederick Douglass's first impressions of New Bedford, Massachusetts, when he arrived there, fresh out of slavery, before the Civil War. There was no warm welcome, no inclusion into society, and no help in adjusting to freedom. There was, however, almost immediately a job that paid enough to make savings possible, and there were no restrictions on his owning property. Since Douglass had been trained as a calker in the Baltimore shipyards (there his wages went to his master), his skills had immediate value in the busy whaling port. All his dignity as a human being, as he himself perceived it with a certain confused and

---

3. The Dred Scott case determined that slaves could not be regarded as US citizens and could not be afforded protection from the federal government or the courts. They could be bought and sold as merchandise. *Dred Scott v. Sanford*, 60 U.S. 393 (1857). —Ed.

ambivalent gratitude, was in his marketable skills, and then in his right to possess whatever property he could accumulate through the sale of those skills. In a real sense, Frederick Douglass was the archetype of the Lockean man. Born a slave, he was able, through his most remarkably adaptive behavior (perhaps the most complex human behavior on historical record), to slip out of slavery and to work himself into the ideological mainstream of America where he became a shaping force and ended up a kind of national elder statesman. Throughout all this he records no relationship with any white person that goes beyond the functional or the ideological, and yet the most creative years of his adult life were spent with whites. He was, in the great Lockean tradition, a formidable loner, and the Lockean tradition rewarded him for his capacity to bear his isolation.

The Civil War, then, was a critical symptom of the breakdown of the Lockean consensus. The great danger it turned out, in defining humans in functional terms, is that they cease to have any value that makes them essentially different from domestic animals or machines. But even beyond this, the nascent scientism in the Lockean ideology requires of those who accept it a passionate belief in doubt. This may be logically impossible, but it is humanly quite possible, and it is currently the only way that humans have of accepting their animal origins, for doubt is a highly effective way of distancing oneself from the whole of creation. Unfortunately, it distances one from other humans, as well. A passionate belief in doubt makes any individual into God, the arbiter of reality. As the Colt Sidearm Firearms Company used to advertise in the 1870s, "Abe Lincoln may have freed all men, but Sam Colt made all men equal." Perhaps John Locke would have been more accurate. Or, even more accurately, "John Locke and Sam Colt make all men equally divine."

It was, then, into the shattered Lockean consensus that followed the Civil War that Spencer's Social Darwinism arrived to such an astonishing welcome. Lodge would say that Social Darwinism simply confirmed and reconstituted the five principles of Lockean ideology. It is true that Social Darwinism was not in conflict with any of these points, but it added a radically new dimension to the first principle: individualism. For Spencer, individuality did *not* derive from the concept of an individual soul, indestructible and immortal. What legitimatized individualism within the Social Darwinist scheme was species survival. Charles Wilson could say, "What is good for General Motors is good for the country,"[4] only because Spencer had claimed that what was good for the most fit individual was good for the species. In this the whole dimension of the corporate, lacking in Locke, was supplied. Whichever team staggers out of the cosmic Super Bowl at the end of time will find themselves as the perfect society. In a sense, Spencer exposes Locke's God, and who is He, after all, but nature, curiously concerned with the perfection of the human species, but hardly concerned with the salvation of individual souls.

Salvation is not for a particular race, or a particularly good person. One need not even accept Jesus' self-definition or even believe what Jesus says about himself. It is enough to look at Jesus' total life, the loving, healing and reconciling quality of it and trust it. From this point forward no person must ever despair of salvation. There is room for all, and it is God's will that all shall follow and find their ultimate home in Him.

Snow and Furnish, *Proclamation*, 37.

By making species survival the first priority, even the basis for the importance of individualism, Spencer managed subtly to change or render more relative the other Lockean principles. Equality comes to mean, simply, equal access to a competing team, the opportunity to test one's fitness. It was after Spencer that the playing fields of Eton took on their metaphoric importance, and

---

4. "Engine" Charles Wilson, president of General Motors, made this statement in 1953 during a Congressional hearing on his nomination. President Eisenhower had proposed Wilson to become Secretary of Defense. —Ed.

team sports in America began to become popular. In America, everyone has an equal right to try out for Little League.

The right of contract is even more relativized within the Social Darwinist scheme, where contracts cease to hold immediately when the survival (for survival read *success, growth, victory*) of either party appears to be in jeopardy. Where adaptive behavior is at the heart of surviving natural selection, all options must be left open. Where a contract is useful, it is observed. Where either party begins to perceive it as maladaptive, it is renegotiated or ignored by the threatened party (i.e. *cost overruns on government–business–military contracts*).

Competition remains, for Spencer, the central mechanism of natural selection, but far from accomplishing the happy societal equilibrium that Locke envisioned, it results in a dynamic movement toward the perfect or "ideal" society. The intelligently aggressive are the most adaptive in competitive terms. Individuals are still, as in the traditional Lockean ideology, in competition with one another, but since the Social Darwinist system is dynamic and moving towards a social ideal rather than individual fulfillment, competition between individuals is subordinate to the purpose of making the team more competitive, so that in the end the species will be perfected. Psychoanalyst Michael Maccoby, in *The Gamesman*, portrays Social Darwinist man to perfection when he describes top corporate management. It is the person who competes with peers for leadership, and, in his first management position, quickly and effectively creates a successful competitive team— competitive, that is, with other teams within the corporation and always for the good of the corporation. Top management, gamesmen like himself, spot his managerial skill and eventually let him into the top to manage the competition with other corporations. His primary motivation is neither money nor power, Dr. Maccoby tells us, but the love of winning and the terror of losing.

Property within the Social Darwinist scheme is quite important, but its significance is utterly changed while remaining metaphysically similar. Property in the Lockean sense is a solid, trustworthy, owned piece of land, an estate, a business, or an industry that generates a good livelihood. However, to the Social Darwinist eye, this is a maladaptive closing of options.

For the Social Darwinist, property is a means of communicating survival status. Money is clearly the most adaptive form of property, and invested money signaled the highest level of survival status, a winner. Such a person may very well buy a country estate and have it farmed, if that is currently what winners are doing, and he will run his farm to his profit by making sure that the farm loses money which can be written off on his income tax. In this way, he signals his aggressive "at-home-ness" with a complex economic system. He will also sell his estate in a minute if estates suddenly lose their sharp symbolic definition. Whatever he owns, he owns for its *symbolic* importance.

Yet in another, metaphorical sense, his ownership of property serves a similar psychological function as the one served actually within the Lockean scheme, in distancing the owner from his neighbor and from the government. The mark of a true winner is his utter disregard for the value of any possession apart from its relationship to his status as a winner, one fit to survive.

Anyone who seriously wants to make sense out of his or her life suspects that what Jesus said, what He did, and the new dimension He added to history, has a powerful current of truth to it. Following His teaching gives me a sense of meaningfulness, importance, and value both of the activity of individuals and the corporate activity of humans. I also feel that what I do myself is important both for myself and for others. I believe that this whole business is very important to God. I believe that one can make a difference by the lovely act of being born.

From a sermon preached at Christ Church,
Cambridge, MA, November 1, 1976.

THE SHIFT FROM SALVATION TO SURVIVAL

Spencer, himself, was for the absolute minimum of government, but Social Darwinism in America obeyed its own inner logic more than did its founder. Beginning with a kind of adversarial, competitive relationship, government and the corporations moved to a radically symbiotic relationship under the survival threat of World War II. The two cooperated to assure that America survived in the natural selection of nations. Since World War II, the corporations have been competing teams within, so to speak, the National Corporation / government. A true survivor, a true winner, moves easily between the corporation and the government where he tries to make sure that the corporations compete just enough to keep them "on their toes" without creating a situation which endangers the capacity of the nation to compete in the arena of nations. The dictates of Social Darwinism made this fading of the boundaries between the corporation and the government inevitable with their emphasis on species survival leading progressively toward species perfection.

Another reordering of Lockean values that took place within the advent of Social Darwinism was the emphasis on science. This was particularly true in America where there was considerable confusion between a scientist and an inventor. Locke, and his two most prominent American disciples, Thomas Jefferson and Benjamin Franklin, were strong advocates of a scientific, empirical approach to life in general. But they had no concept of science as an institution separate from other human institutions, save perhaps that of medicine. Lewis Thomas, in a 1973 speech to the American Academy for the Advancement of Science, observed that, in colonial America, medicine was not scientific beyond a crude empiricism based on trial and error which usually resulted in a therapy that happened precisely in that order.

Within the Social Darwinist scheme, science was to become the cutting edge of progress, a team effort that would result in the ideal society. This inevitably linked science to the social-economic-technological progress of the nation, and / or the species, and science in America ceased to become the obsessive hobby of eccentric individuals and became an established institution in its own right. It slowly took over the attributes of established religion. Yet, as the socio-biologist E. O. Wilson points out, even within science, research took on a highly competitive, adversary dynamic which in time proved rather less than efficient. A paper is published that presents a new theory. A paper appears, in response, to tear it to pieces and presents a counter theory. This encounter generates a flurry of papers defending one theory or the other, and years go by before a working consensus emerges from all this *Sturm und Drang*. The old individualism dies hard.

Efficient or not, the pragmatic link between science, technology, and industry was unquestionably the cause of stunning industrial-technological growth of American society. In good Social Darwinist fashion, America became number one in the cosmic arena of nations. The inefficiency in terms of the wastefulness that a competitive dynamic was bound to generate has yet to be dwelt with. The entire enterprise was founded on the assumption of infinite resources and unlimited growth. Even knowledge began to be regarded as without limits.

Until 1945, science was given an increasingly Messianic role in our evolution toward the ideal society. The dropping of atomic bombs on Hiroshima and Nagasaki called this role into question. In the Manhattan Project, science was called out of the university into the domain of government and industry and made an integral part of both. It had become a major ingredient in the dynamics of political and economic power that shaped the lives of everyone. Even more important, it now seemed that the dilemma into which science had led the human species was a dilemma from which only the little known, privileged, elitist mystique of science could rescue the human species.

Species survival was suddenly not so much a theoretical goal as a hard ugly present issue, the outcome of which was hardly assured. The question, "Who is to survive?," was answered by, "The fittest," and came to mean the powerful with the most critically important scientific-technological information.

It would be impossible to have listened to the 1977 Convention of the American Academy for the Advancement of Science, covered by National Public Radio, without suspecting that the scientific establishment had already concluded that the survival of the species was utterly dependent on its own survival. The lectures at the Academy dealt primarily with what were perceived as crisis areas—energy, agriculture, weather, and, most significantly, the political trials and tribulations of biologists working on recombinant DNA.[5]

Most at issue was the action of the Cambridge, Massachusetts City Council in establishing by law a commission of citizens to monitor recombinant DNA research at Harvard and the Massachusetts Institute of Technology in the area of public safety. Comments on this action were negative. Academia saw the event as ominous, a first step toward what could become a consistent, nation-wide "meddling" of citizens in scientific research. Science, the academy was told more than once, is elitist by its very nature and should be so boldly. The layperson is simply incapable of understanding its complexities and should leave all decisions regarding its direction to scientists.

Indeed, the scientific establishment sounded, in its Lockean-Darwinian dogmatism, very much like business and industrial management inveighing against government interference, and George Ball, former US Ambassador to the United Nations, used

5. While the director of the Federal Government's National Institutes of Health (NIH) prominent research cardiologist, Dr. Donald S. Frederickson, became entangled in a dispute over the scientific discovery of how to hybridize DNA, called "recombinant DNA" (rDNA), in which hybridized strings of DNA could be inserted into viruses and bacteria, thereby changing their structure and action. This discovery was likened to that of Prometheus stealing the secret of fire, and it was feared that, once this gene splicing had begun, unpredictable environmental hazards, such as a resistant strain of E. coli, might threaten the general populace. Did the NIH have the resources and authority to set laboratory standards? This debate entered into the sphere of the laity, and in the summer of 1977, the Cambridge City Council held contentious hearings, created the Cambridge Biohazards Committee, and demanded from the NIH an environmental impact statement. Between 1976 and 1979, twelve bills were introduced into Congress calling for regulation on DNA research ("The Donald S. Fredrickson Papers"). —Ed.

the metaphor of the impediments to industrial growth caused by the government's environmental impact studies as a sign of what science could expect from such interference.

What is important here, one suspects, is how clearly the tacit influence of Spencer alters the role of science in the Lockean consensus. For Locke, as for Jefferson or John Adams, scientific thinking was assumed to take place in a homeostatic, steady-state universe, and its role was to understand this universe, the rules and laws of its working. Its application was for the purpose of facilitating human existence within this naturally—indeed, divinely—ordered system. What exploded this paradigm and made it unworkable as a societal paradigm (even before it was perceived as an unworkable scientific paradigm) was Darwin's evolutionary theory so quickly applied as social evolution or the concept of progress. Adams, conjecturing on the future of America, certainly saw growth as a part of this future, but it was growth toward maturity, in terms of high culture where science, art, poetry, philosophy, and the leisure required to cultivate these humane pursuits would emerge from a just, prosperous, and rational society. The movement of society was toward an equilibrium that would reflect more accurately the rule-bound equilibrium of nature. A government of "laws, not men" puts a very high priority on limits.

The Spencerian concept of the "survival of the fittest" sees all limits unrelated to the survival of an elite as maladaptive. The American scientific establishment generally subscribes to this Spencerian dynamic not simply because it is self-serving, but because it is also consonant with what Albert Einstein and Werner Heisenberg have done to the social paradigm within which it works. Where scientists say, "what can be done will be done," they seem to mean, "what can be done *should* be done."

Scientists, for the most part, are as ethical as any other professional group, and have perhaps been more concerned with ethics since Hiroshima than most professional groups. They are not conspiring to destroy the world, but they do seem to perceive themselves as conspiring to save it. What one questions is whether doing everything and hoping that the most adaptive science will necessarily survive and prevail to rescue the human enterprise, especially when the human enterprise tends to be identified with the scientific enterprise, and the ultra-Spencerian assumptions [underlying those actions and hopes] are validly human.

Scientists, however, are undeniably human. What came through the actual scientific debate that took place before the Cambridge City Council was that the proponents of uncontrolled recombinant DNA research were worried that a "critical breakthrough" in their field would take place somewhere else. Their fear was that if it did take place first in one of the number of other universities where research was proceeding unencumbered rather than at Harvard or MIT, it would render their biology departments "second rate," or "unfit to survive." It was as if the Cambridge City Council was presuming to manage the Harvard football team or the MIT crew.

In respect to this irrational competitiveness, scientists are no different from the rest of us. Ministers, doctors, business people, teachers, poets, novelists, men or women, to the extent that they have been raised and educated or worked in America during the latter quarter of the century, have all experienced pressure to compete which is all out of proportion to what humane existence requires or to what an efficient corporate enterprise requires. We have been corrupted by competition in our marriages, our families, our churches and synagogues, our friendships, our schools and colleges, even our recreation. It is rapidly becoming an assumption of our society that the basic human relationship is *an adversarial one*. We must ask ourselves why this is, why we have fallen back with such a vengeance on a highly questionable, indeed, a discredited apprehension of reality, where only two human categories have significance: winners and losers, survivors and the vanquished.

[Snow continues his observation of how our acceptance of Social Darwinism in American life has diminished individual self-worth as well as threatened the integrity of our country; he then adds the following apology]:

I am attempting to get at the imperialism of competition in many aspects of our institutional and personal lives. Some observations are specifically theological and Christian for various reasons. First, granted that the historical record of Christianity and its involvement in creating, however heretically, the very competitive social ambiance my writings condemn, it is not my intention to offer Christianity, particularly in its institutional forms, as the answer to Social Darwinism.

Second, the very mention of Christianity is likely to call forth precisely the competitive response which comes so naturally to Americans of whatever conscious religious or non-religious persuasion. Indeed, in the Biblical and theological aspects of these observations, I find competitive hidden agenda in myself ringing rather too loud and clear.

Third, I fear that non-Christians will regard these offerings as not for them. I maintain that competitiveness is the "inner demon" that so effectively renders American Socialists politically ineffective. Like the rest of us, Socialists are no better at cooperative behavior for simply believing in Socialism on a conscious level. Granted the current American distrust of cooperation in any form, an American Socialism would probably be brutally authoritarian and based on police terror. We must learn to deal with the survival terror in ourselves before we shall be capable of any cooperative social organization that is not fascist. I believe that the same thing is true for some of those whose passion for ecology has currently taken on religious dimensions. Many of the communards of yesteryear are homesteaders today. I would hope that what I have written could be for anyone who is concerned about irrational competition in our society.

And yet the theological-Biblical parts *are* included, in part because they provide a needed vocabulary and add an alternate perspective to the kind of empiricism which is, in part, responsible for our dilemma. I wish I could say that they are included because they reflect my customary way of thinking, but that is only very partially the case. My customary way of thinking is the same as any other middle-class American's: empirical, pragmatic, competitive, and individualistic. If the theological-Biblical portions of my writing are clumsy and simplistic, they still, in my opinion, provide access to another way of looking at reality. In the end, I join with Peter Elbow and hope that the reader will read these reflections as an owl eats a mouse. Just swallow it whole and let the organism sort it out.[6]

6. Elbow, *Writing Without Teachers*, 177.

2

Education and the New Social Darwinism

THE WISDOM OF THE WORKING CLASS

When I was eighteen during the first year of World War II, I was rejected by the armed forces. If this happened to an eighteen-year-old in 1966, he would have regarded himself declared "fit to survive" and quite possibly have engineered that rejection himself. It was not so in 1941. I felt rejected by the human race.[1] In a devastating depression, I signed up as a laborer at the Pearl Harbor Navy Yard. Transportation for civilian workers was slow in those days, and I spent three months working at Mare Island Navy Yard in Vallejo, California, waiting for a boat. I was assigned to a crew of outside riggers, mostly men in their forties and fifties from Oklahoma or Arkansas, driven with their families to California by The Dust Bowl and The Great Depression.

---

1. In 1943 John Snow was accepted into the United States Navy as a "Medic." —Ed.

I had had two years of accelerated studies in college before I began my two years as a workingman. I was a small, rather frail person raised in a quiet, middle-class suburb. I was at first frightened by these generally huge, older working-class men. I expected them to be crude and dumb. A few were crude. Most were stable family men, and most were smart indeed. So smart that ideas, supervision, or hierarchies were unknown. Outside rigging is a job of moving things into place which are too heavy for a few men to handle, and is consequently an *ad hoc* sort of trade. Using anything from block and tackle to a Gantry crane, the rigger, or a gang of riggers, gets everything from a painter's scaffold to whole sections of a ship into place. Some jobs are simple horse work; others are very complex and precise. Each job is different; only the gear remains the same. The best rigger, it was agreed, was weak and lazy. He uses his intelligence and his tools, not his muscles.

On the gang to which I was assigned, some of the men had learned rigging in the oil fields, some in lumbering, some had been ship's riggers all of their adult lives, but fully half had learned the trade within the last two years, having a background in farming or as cowhands. The astonishing thing was that everyone seemed to know how to do everything about equally well. Rating was based on seniority. The longer one worked for the Civil Service, the more pay you made. But vary rarely did any authority go with the rating. The "snapper," our immediate boss, did the liaison work with other trades, but that was in addition to working with us at whatever we were about. He never told us how to do our job. There was no need to; everyone seemed to know.

A propeller shaft for an aircraft carrier is both very heavy and very fragile. The fine tolerances of the shaft can't be bruised in any way. It can be lowered easily enough into a dry dock by crane, but unfortunately it's installed under the fantail, so that it must be positioned and positioned perfectly from below for the outside machinists to install it. Riggers improvise scaffolding and artfully position chain falls and blocks. They do this, all the while trying to keep the machinists and ship superintendents from having a nervous breakdown. Although I saw my gang do this several times, it is hard to describe how. No one "took charge." An incredible amount of body language went on. Verbal suggestions were quickly accepted or rejected, not by discussion or vote, but by moving together to implement the suggestion, or by not moving at all, as if the suggestion had never been made. The ideal was the same as the scientific ideal: to find the simplest possible solution to a complex problem. Then there would be a moment of truth, the shaft stymied a few inches from where it could be fitted by the machinists, when a rigger would sense some mystical point of leverage, step forward with a board which he happened to notice on the ground, give one exquisite pry and the shaft would be in place. We would all cheer and applaud, albeit ironically.

Riggers loaf a lot. They have to wait for the use of a crane, or to be assigned to a new job. They smoke and talk. The talk was the best I've ever known. It was usually anecdotal, but seldom aimlessly so. We were engaged in a continual definition of life. When Eric Hoffer says that the working class people are "lumpy with creativity," he meant *that* generation. They were. Of ten men, five were members of the United Iron Workers' Union. One of these was enthusiastic about it. He was a Marxist, a heavy reader, an ideologue in his sixties much respected by us all. The other four regarded their union as a necessary evil. The other five hated unions. All loved Roosevelt, including the Marxist.

But mainly our reflections were philosophical. Some of the men, beside the Marxist, were readers. All read the newspapers. A discussion would begin with a story from the newspaper of the previous day which had described some human dilemma: a bank robbery, an airplane crash, a murder, the divorce of a celebrity, a corrupt draft board, a labor dispute, etc. The men would respond to such a story with anecdotes from their own lives, often followed by brief abstract philosophical or moral conclusions.

The philosophical consensus seemed at first to reveal a deep cynicism. Life was not all as it presented itself, or as it was presented in the media. One phrase recurred continually: "Don't never trust nobody." Yet, the anecdotal material, as it became cumulative day after day, was often in contradiction to this philosophical statement. The anecdotes, which could, on occasion, take on near epic proportions and be told with consummate skill, reflected not a cynical but a tragic view of life. It was not that people were consciously devious, not that they were liars or manipulative, or deceitful (although such characters were often in the anecdotes as protagonists). It was that every human being had a dark side, impulsive, destructive, self-destructive, and irrational, which would on occasion assert itself powerfully with tragic consequences. In the end, these men believed, life was not rational or predictable; it was extremely dangerous with as much of the danger within oneself as in one's ambient world.

Knowing this was, for them, the essence of being mature, trustworthy, knowledgeable, and of good judgment. It was their conviction that going to college worked against such knowledge. A college graduate was convinced once and for all that life was rational, could be controlled, and made to work for the betterment of oneself and the world. It was for this reason that they regarded a college graduate as a "fool."

But these men did not regard life as just dangerous. It was also mysterious, full of ironic justice, hilarious discontinuity and paradox, and stunning but significant betrayals. Indeed, the anecdotal definition of reality, they believed, could lead a person to enough wisdom and judgment to meet life with dignity and a degree of serenity. Woven into all this was a code, defined more in action than in words. One never turned down a person in trouble who needed money or food or whatever help one could give, even if the person was notoriously unreliable. One never accepted any form of hierarchical bullying. If one had an overbearing and abusive boss, one told him off, even if it meant being fired or having to quit. One always repaid a personal loan. One never overpromised, and one promised carefully, but one kept one's word. (The essence of being a college graduate, they believed, was that while they were apt to overpromise and failed at keeping their word, they were unaware of doing either.) One always showed up at work, whether hung-over, sick, physically hurt, or whatever. The only excuse for not showing up was the utter physical inability to get there. One never stole. Theft meant immediate social excommunication. One never betrayed a confidence or bragged.

Looked at systematically, the code was a set of negative feedback devices to maintain a viable equilibrium in a group where relationships were basically symmetrical and non-hierarchical. Hostility was handled by kidding, a kind of heavy irony where annoying behavior on the part of one person would be immediately caricatured by several peers. They might say, in the event that a hung-over rigger would not be carrying his fair share of rigging gear from the shop to the job, something like, "The king here would like you peons to carry the chain falls this morning, as he is indisposed." "Oh, sorry, your majesty. We didn't hear about the royal celebration last night." The riggers saw both work and life as a *corporate* enterprise. All that made life bearable, from their point of view, was that an individual gave his consent to the human endeavor in which he was involved. In the process of giving his consent he would come to understand it, and in his understanding of it, he would become free. Within this rigging gang, and, generally within working class America until after World War II, all real authority came with the abdication of competitiveness and personal ambition.

I wonder if learning to love is not, in the end, letting grace triumph over law in our hearts. This has an analogy in sports. When we learn any sport, we are awkward and clumsy at first as we try to remember all the rules, most of them in their negative form. "Don't bend your left arm, your hand's too far over the shaft, you looked up, you didn't follow through. Look at the ball."

But for most people there comes a time when the rules, negative and positive, are built into the action, a time when all the golfer's concentration is on the green, all the skier's concentration is on the slope, all the hunter's concentration is on the bird, the fly-fisherman's concentration on the trout. There comes a time when the particular laws of action become subordinate to the forms of action, and the

awkwardness and hesitancy and tentativeness of the begin-
ner give way to the graceful commitment of the expert. The
real expert begins to break rules right and left. He or she
goes beyond good form to achieve a personal style, discov-
ering the way they perform best. But the most important
moment, the moment of transition from law to grace, is
precisely the moment when a person ceases to try to do the
right thing, when a person stops thinking about himself /
herself doing the thing, and moves his / her attention to the
object of doing.

Love is like this. We must learn the Ten Command-
ments. We must, at first, learn not to steal, or lie, or murder,
or covet, and the rest. We must learn, in fact, to control
ourselves. But if this is as far as we go, then most of our
energy goes into controlling ourselves, and trying unsuc-
cessfully to control the world. St. Paul reminds us that as we
try to stamp out our wrong impulses, anything upsetting
in ourselves or the world around us, they pop up in new
disguises. Then there comes that mystical moment in the
life of each of us, when The Law is built into our actions.
It is as if one is confirmed, as if someone or some group or
society, so to speak, puts its hands on your head and says,
"You are whole. You're fine. You have value. You're free.
Now *love*! When this happens, we enter a whole new order
of existence.

But we also must remember that this is an ongoing process. With each crisis in confidence in a person's life, there
is a falling back upon The Law. There is a need to quit jus-
tifying and protecting ourselves and to start loving again.
And it is here that the sports analogy ends. None of us will
learn to love as well as Sugar Ray Robinson fights, or as
successful as Ted Williams at bat. All human love is simple,
awkward, habitual, reflective, intelligent, accomplished,
and clumsy. There are no world champions at Christian
love, because there's no competition. Their many forms
reflect the rich variety of human love that adds energy and

spirit to the world and transforms it. When we love, we're all on the same team.

From a sermon preached at Christ Church, Cambridge, MA, February 13, 1966.

Among these ten men I guess that IQs would have ranged from 100 to 140. But intelligence itself was not the possession, the property, of an individual. The intelligence of the less intelligent was shared with and accepted gracefully by the more intelligent. It contributed to a common pool of intelligence which was accessible to all, and, indeed, essential to the human enterprise of life and work. Intelligence was spread around, and there turned out to be a lot of it.

It was a surprise to me that this group of men was not more individualistic. I had a pioneer stereotype for Westerners, and these men, although they did verbal obeisance before the shrine of individualism on occasion, simply didn't live up to the stereotype. But this, too, got dealt with anecdotally. They had gone the road of rugged individualism, some of them passionately, as young men. They had begun trying to out-drink, out-fight, and out-work everybody in the world. Having survived this wildness, they had gone for the independence of farming or ranching, saving until they could make a down payment on their own spread. This independence was wiped out by the Depression and drought, and some found themselves in California as migrant workers picking vegetables. Their experience had made them distrustful of ambition and nourished their belief in one's responsibility for one's neighbor. For a few, this belief was an explicitly Christian one. For most, it was simply the logic of experience. For these men, survival was not so much a goal but a miracle, an unexplainable day-to-day gift over which they had very limited control. The goal of life was to be trustworthy in whatever one was called to do. They would have agreed with Freud. The point is to love and to work.

God and love are not management tools; they will not do what we tell them to do. But strangely enough, force is not as useful as it seems, either. Sure, it gets the job done, if by "the job" we mean the handling of discrete symptoms of social or institutional disorder. But there always seem to be the after-effects of force. These can be the unexpected failure of morale, outbursts of cruelty and revenge, or new surprising disruptions of the system. To fix or solve these verbs implies a forceful management of reality, a domination and control over existence that makes us, as human beings, masters of our environment. They are arrogant words, even as they apply to the world of things. Applied to the world of persons they go beyond arrogance to become violent words.

Let's think of the world of things for the moment. The first important thing I had to learn as a ship's rigger was how to splice wire rope. The rigger I was assigned to carefully showed me how it was done. You took a marlin spike, inserted it into the wire in such a way as to lift up one of the six strands, twisted the spike up to a spot where it was convenient to tuck one of the working strands through, and then run the strand down into place.

I tried for fifteen minutes to insert the spike into the wire. Finally the rigger handed me a four-pound mallet. "Here, try this!" I pounded away for another fifteen minutes without making a dent in the wire. "There," said the rigger, "that's your first lesson. You can't make a wire rope do what you want it to do. You have to learn from it what it will and won't do. You have to learn from the spike what it will and won't do and can't do. You have to let it teach your hands. Your hands have to learn to pay attention, to be taught. For them to obey you, you must learn to obey them."

Now, this wasn't a Zen master talking, this was a rigger, a small man and a master teacher. He taught me that the one thing I had to know to learn a trade: Humility. Humility must be practiced in the presence of things. Intelligence was to no avail. Strength was to no avail. The key was a curious kind of obedience to reality itself.

Brother David Steindl-Rast,[2] a Benedictine monk, once said something to the effect that obedience has always meant to listen completely. It is the utter giving of one's attention (in my case giving the hands' attention) that constitutes obedience. So, there in the rigging loft, I had learned a trade secret that turned out to be one of the basic principles of Christianity.

Only later did I apply it to faith. The reason one practices obedience is to serve. Serving is the Christian alternative to using force, to fixing, to solving, to winning or surviving. It is the reason we are here, to serve God and to serve love, not to make others do what we want them to do. If we are to serve God we must listen completely, and that means to be utterly open, utterly undefended, and, finally, utterly vulnerable. This kind of service involves suffering, but it will be suffering we have chosen. If we do not listen to our neighbor, how will we be able to hear the voice of our creator?

From a sermon preached at Christ Church,
Cambridge, MA, January 9, 1977.

EXCELLENCE AND SURVIVAL

Well, so much for the wisdom of the working class. The sons of a number of these men were also in the service. The sons of many more men like these men were also in the service. When they left the service they were eligible for the GI Bill of Rights. Many of them took advantage of that eligibility and went to college or to

2. David Steindl-Rast was raised and educated in Vienna. He immigrated to the United States and, in 1953, entered Mt. Savior Benedictine monastery in Elmira, NY. Thirteen years later he became involved in Buddhist–Christian dialogues. In 1968, he co-founded the Center for Spiritual Studies. He is the author of nine books on spirituality, and divides his time between lecturing worldwide and living as a senior member of Mt. Savior in a hermitage. —Ed.

graduate school. After World War II the ranks of the middle class swelled. One could go to school and be paid a living at the same time. A college degree became the norm for many Americans.

The GI Bill was a generous and imaginative social experiment enabling countless thousands of people to live up to their intellectual capacities fully. But there is never any pure gain in education. It had sociological and psychological costs. One cost was obvious. The working class lost its leadership. Whereas before, intelligence and competence were spread evenly across all economic classes to the extent that Americans could claim a kind of classlessness apart from the economic sphere, but since the war, working class men and women had gone to college and moved into a totally different world from that in which they had been raised. This new world was changing so rapidly that it had *no* clear definition. The goals of the new American middle class were defined mainly through advertising: one must get ahead and one must consume. The rest slowly fell into place.

Before World War II, the public schools served a dual function. They were the primary vehicles of the "melting pot," an opportunity for different classes to get to know one another, and become "good citizens" as they learned basic skills, but they were also a sorting out place. Larger high schools had courses with emphases that depended far more on actual achievement in the particular school system than on standardized testing. There would be the "college course," the "commercial course," and the "manual arts course." Students were more often permitted to choose their course than they were "guided" into a track the school thought appropriate. Standardized tests were used, but their purpose was the generally benign one of finding out where a child was so that he or she could be taught what he or she did not know. No thought was given to using them for teacher accountability or as a final definition of a child's achievement level. It was a useful educational system. Good school achievers were usually well taught whether they were in the college course or not, and the socialization, though achieving no real blending of ethnic cultures or a classless society, did succeed in providing enough ideological consensus to make political democracy viable. Public school teachers in small towns and rural areas were usually the most intelligent women in the area. Some had a couple of years in teacher's colleges, but it was simply considered logical that intelligent and competent women should teach children. In many larger towns and small cities these women were cultivated graduates of four-year colleges. There was no issue of status. A teacher was a personage, a professional person.

But, years later, when comedian Bob Hope maintained that the reason Mr. Khrushchev, on his visit to the United States, was not permitted to Disneyland was because that was the only place we had a rocket that worked, he was the only one who laughed. The American reaction to Sputnik, the first space satellite, was bizarre. We blamed our "failure" to be "number one" in rocketry on our poor public school system where science was badly taught. There was, the theory went, too much emphasis on "socialization" and not enough on "excellence." No one quite knew what *excellence* meant, but everyone snapped to attention. To *excel* is not to do something well, it is to do something far better than anyone else. "Excellence" is not a goal but a *gift from on high*, as the Latin root informs us. To strive after excellence is a contradiction in terms. In practice, however, the excellence that received as much money, energy, and scientific attention in our public schools was excellence in its pure form. By use of standardized tests the nation determined in absolutely quantified terms who the "excellent" were and pitted these against one another from an early age.

Those determined to be excellent were, of course, largely white and middle class, the children of college graduates generated by the GI Bill. No one seemed to give much thought about what should be done with the less talented students. Those who couldn't cope with physics, those who found their text books not sufficiently relevant to their lives to make them see *why* one learned to read, all those were left to thrash around in school taught by people who felt frustrated at having to teach them. In the process, education evolved into determining the winners and the losers. The basic educational flaw in the new Social Darwinism is its assumption that intelligence is private property and competitively marketable.

Education regarded in this way believed that intelligence will rise to the top if sufficiently motivated by money and status. What was lost was the concept that the whole purpose of learning is to *make sense* out of one's life, one's corporate life, and one's life as an individual.

Millions were spent in the late fifties to change the image of science. Polls had revealed that many children had regarded scientists as "mad." However mad the scientists may have been, the educational social engineers must have been totally mad, judging by the results of their experiment. It was soon discovered that our rockets didn't fly not because of a faulty educational system, but for subtle acoustical reasons easily dealt with once diagnosed. Our rockets began to fly like crazy. The educational system was not so fortunate. Professional female teachers, who had been the backbone of the public educational system and exemplified a humane attitude toward all levels of students, were beginning to take their place in other, more lucrative professions such as law, medicine, college teaching, and real estate. In their place appeared some careerist men with their eyes on the top administrative jobs and a great many women bored with keeping the house who liked the extra money.

Thus education's new momentum toward excellence from top to bottom ultimately succeeded in producing the most alienated, isolated, confused population of university students in history. The ultimate moment of Social Darwinism (the new government regulated Social Darwinism) came when a deferment from the draft was made to those who went to college or for those who would agree to do graduate work in areas deemed valuable to the nation, namely areas related to national defense. Secretary McNamara said quite plainly that using the draft in this way would supply the technological and social leadership for the future while keeping underclass youths out of the job market and providing them with some basic work skills. With Vietnam, education was perceived (by those being educated) as quite literally a struggle to survive. Those who got into college could prepare themselves for the good life; those who didn't were guaranteed a year in Vietnam. Defining the categories of winners and losers became the central purpose of American education, and it continues to be its central purpose to this day. *Excellence* is a code word for Social Darwinism.

With the pressure of excellence pervading the educational domain, some parents opted to send their children to private schools to ensure their child's success. These children were faced with their first set of aptitude tests, the SSATs. These exams, under whatever condition they are taken, create their own competitive ambience. The parents see the SSATs as prefiguring the ultimate moment of truth, the PSATs and SATs or the College Boards. The young people fated to take these exams are often anxious out of all proportion to the importance of these exams in helping private school admissions officers to select their next year's entering class. A kind of mini-apocalypse occurs. This experience is finally chalked up to a "rehearsal for the kind of pressure they will have to take later." This is not helpful to the bright kid who has, as they say, "choked."

This whole experience (doubled in spades when it is repeated as SATs) removed the last vestiges of true learning from the educational process. None of it, in its meaninglessly quantified results, made any sense at all except in Social Darwinist terms. One was assigned a number, and one is too often convinced that one's total worth is defined in terms of that number. In graduate school one would hear a remark like, "Her problem is that she's a 690 person in a 750 world."

The IQ, the quantification of intelligence, never had the same power to damage the ego that the SAT has, mainly because it wasn't generally told to the child and seldom told to his or her parents. The children would often get the message that they were regarded as "dull normal" but never suffered the painful trauma of opening an envelope to discover that the Educational Testing Service of Princeton, New Jersey, had declared them unlikely to achieve at a college level, or unlikely to handle the work at a "first-rate" college, or, in some cases just as alienating, declared them to be in the 98th percentile of all students in America and doomed to another eight years of trying to cut the throats of that other two percent. The basic assumption behind the massive use of the Educational Testing Service is the neo-Darwinist one; again, that intelligence is private property that is competitively marketable. SATs and GREs and the various specialized tests for professional schools are all reductionist attempts to determine the market value of one's working intelligence. The numbers are indicators of the value of one's working intelligence in a competitive market. As such they are quite useful to large, impersonal institutions that are obsessively concerned with their own survival, institutions which are often surprisingly candid in describing their own inner life as a *jungle*, namely, the universities. Dr. Michael Maccoby, in his book *The Gamesman*, maintains that the most amoral and ruthlessly in-dividualistic gamesman, whom he describes as the "jungle fighter," is usually the academic entrepreneur, the professor, not the busi-ness or industrial manager who has to maintain some semblance of team work.[3]

Viewed historically, this is not surprising. No other institu-tion was so quick as academia to embrace Herbert Spencer, prob-ably the most important single shaping force in sociology, and a key influence in the early days of academic psychology. No other institution so unashamedly pits individual against individual in such naked competition, and unashamedly insists that this is the most effectual educational method. The universities have supplied us with our most Social Darwinist public servants in recent years. Unlike business and individual managers and other competitive types who have simply swallowed Social Darwinist assumptions unreflectively, the university, particularly the scientific and social scientific establishment, has a growing number of articulate true believers. And sure enough, their battle cry is "excellence." One example of this kind of academic thinking may be found in "A Letter to the Faculty on Undergraduate Education," a document published in 1974 having to do with curriculum revision at Har-vard. Dean Henry Rosovski, its author, states:

---

3. Maccoby describes the source of this fighter's energy as being a "lust for power and pleasure in crushing his opponent" (*The Gamesman*, 105). —Ed.

> In the end we may hope to achieve not merely a more
> rational basis for the allocation of our resources in the
> difficult years ahead, but a renewed vitality and distinc-
> tion in the intellectual atmosphere of the college. This ef-
> fort is mandatory if we are to maintain the preeminence
> of education and justify its costliness.[4]

Note the word *preeminence* where "quality" might have done
just as well. Note that preeminence is to justify its costliness. In
simple terms, this dean was saying that if Harvard is to survive,
it will need enough money to guarantee its preeminence, or that
only its preeminence will guarantee enough money for its survival.
In whatever case, there is no better way to prove a college's preeminence than by *quantifying it*. One can say that more of its graduates
get into the "best" professional schools, or that its graduates do
better (get better grades) in professional schools, or one can say
that graduates score higher on the Graduate Record Exam, or the
LSAT, or whatever, but the minute one starts thinking in competitive terms of preeminence, one starts thinking in quantified terms
of the bottom line. The minute a university sees its goal as being
better than other universities, it loses its capacity truly to educate,
truly to help students make sense of their lives. It begins to haze
its students, rank its students, make courses "harder" (whatever
that means . . . longer reading lists?), create competitive tensions
between and within departments, create preposterous obstacles
to its doctorates, and generally to create a careerist atmosphere
which precludes any serious learning. It does teach one big thing,
however: how to think strategically, how to calculate, how to keep
one's options open. It also teaches how to survive in the pathetic,
paranoid, destructive style of the committed Social Darwinist. It
turns out, as my friends on the rigging gang suspected, a considerable number of fools.

The hope of the world, according to Christian scripture, is
not to be found in the mainstream with its leaders' illusions

4. Henry Rosovsky, "A Letter to the Faculty on Undergraduate Education."
(Unpublished manuscript, October 1974) 2.

of omnipotence, but among the marginal whom the Hebrew prophets identified as the poor, the captive, the sick, the blind, and the oppressed. Jesus came out of that tradition which demanded compassion and fair treatment for the marginal. But Jesus took it a step further. Jesus himself was a marginal person, a person on the fringe of Nazarene society. For Jesus, the margin rather than the mainstream was the primary concern of God. Out of the rich chaos of its poverty, its pain, its illness, its anger, its excommunication, its hunger, and, in a curious way, its bonded-ness, its wisdom, its understanding of life stripped bare of illusion and lived in the hard light of its fragility and mortality, came the salvation of the world, the Messiah, Jesus. And he tried to teach us that being on the margins is not a result of bad luck or bad genes or ineptitude or criminal behavior or economic trends; marginality is part of the human condition. It is a universal experience of human beings. It is in *the acceptance* of our marginality that the hope lives. Our marginality is a condition of our mortality. We do not own the world; we are sojourners here, here briefly for a few years to share the human condition.

These days, more and more people are being pushed to the margins by the high tech, prosperous, thriving mainstream. Farmers, industrial workers, children, the elderly, single parents, refugees, and so on are all pushed to the edge of the mainstream and abandoned. While it seems as though life is one long struggle to avoid the margin, it is really one long struggle *toward* the margin. When we understand this, we begin to look at life differently, by praying for and living for the transformation of the mainstream, by asking them to move from fear and distrust to repentance. Asking them to take a new and different look at the human condition with all its marginality and to see it as something good, intended and created by God sustained and animated by the Holy Spirit. This way of looking at life mitigates our fears of marginality, and our fear of death, making us better equipped than many to cope with the danger and

disorder of our time. It brings about our kindness, acceptance, forgiveness, and compassion and love that resurrects
and endures.

From a sermon preached at Christ Church,
Cambridge, MA, October 18, 1987.

3

Social Darwinism
and Racial Justice

At some point in early 1965, William Buckley debated James Baldwin at Cambridge University. Although I can't remember what the debate was about, I do remember that, early on, Buckley said that extensive, worldwide research in human intelligence had showed decisively that blacks were less intelligent than whites. Baldwin shrugged his shoulders and said, in effect, something like this: "I'm not a social scientist and I haven't heard about the study you refer to. I suppose it could be right. I suppose that whites could be more intelligent than blacks, or maybe blacks could be more intelligent than whites, but I don't see what difference it makes. It's my belief that both blacks and whites are human and have a right to equal justice."

For a moment Buckley, the most articulate of humans, was speechless. His jaw dropped. His eyes were uncomprehending. Buckley, who was no more a racist than anyone else, but a mischievous debater, thought he had delivered the ultimate racial insult and obviously expected Baldwin to explode and be thereafter utterly irrational, an old debater's trick. Quite the opposite happened. Baldwin, with a simple statement, had questioned the assumption upon which Buckley's total apprehension of reality was based—that intelligence is the most important thing about being human.

If we forget Spencer and his dubious social science for a moment and look at natural selection from a modern socio-biological point of view, we discover that a socio-biologist regards the most important thing about a human or any other living creature is that it carries the genes of its species. The important thing, important in its interconnectedness to the total economy of the biosphere, is the high potential for continuing adaptive characteristics in the pool of genes that recreates the species from generation to generation. Spencer, along with Malthus and Adam Smith, tended to regard intelligent aggression, or competitive intelligence, as the primary adaptive characteristic for survival.

CORPORATE ALTRUISM VS. COMPETITIVE LANGUAGE

E. O. Wilson sees adaptive behavior as far more complex than simple aggressive competition, however intelligent. Among the most "successful" social insects and animals, a high degree of what Wilson calls "altruism" is a critically important dimension of their survival. Altruism for Wilson is a sort of genetic compulsion to cooperate at adaptive tasks leading to species survival.

Wilson is particularly taken with a kind of African termite [*macrotermitinae*] that on its own is no great shaker and with a few peers tends to be hardly more than actively confused. But when some mystical number of these termites get together, in the presence of their favorite building material, they turn into a collective version of Leonardo Da Vinci, Frank Lloyd Wright, and Buckminster Fuller. Presumably, they all put their little heads together and work out an incredibly complex adaptive response to their environment that involves building an elaborate structure based on arches. It is also efficiently air-conditioned. This is not an intelligent response to an environmental challenge, but it is more intelligent than anything that Americans have worked out so far in terms of housing. But it is not a conscious response. They don't know what they are doing. They are, simply, obedient to their genes; in touch with their special DNA, they are brilliantly programmed. It seems unlikely that they are competing with another construction team for some architectural prize.

What humans have substituted for, or have been given in place of this direct programming of their behavior, is language. The most important thing about humans is that they talk. Or, I suppose I could say that the most programmed aspect of human behavior is communication through language, spoken and written. Humans are obedient, for the most part, to what they are told. In the beginning, at least in the human beginning, was *The Word*. Words made for a very complicated form of communication. As Walker Percy points out, bees communicate too.[1] One little winged messenger who has struck it rich communicates it by an elaborate dance which indicates where the pollen is. But, as Percy says, he can't lie. He can't send all his co-workers off on a wild-goose chase while he goes back to enjoy his prize in solitary ecstasy. Adam, once he had partaken of the fruit of the tree of knowledge, started lying, and he wasn't the last human to do so. Language puts us at one remove from our genetic tapes. It takes on a life of its own (to tyrannize as well as to serve the human endeavor), yet it is all we have to tell us who we are and what we are supposed to do. IQ tests may measure our ability to use language, but not our willingness to tell the truth.

Language also puts us at one remove from the world we use to describe and manipulate. There can often be a considerable discrepancy between what we describe and what actually happened when we do not intend to lie. The world, it turns out, is rather more complex than the symbol system, the language we have for understanding and coping with it. Language is not reality, but a complicated code we devise for understanding and coping with what is going on. This distance which language puts between us and reality makes us extraordinarily adaptive, but since it takes us sixteen years to use the language effectively, and, for a genius,

1. Percy, *The Message in the Bottle*, 304.

perhaps thirty years to master it, language can become a very mal-adaptive mode of survival behavior.

Take DDT. Insects who are born smart and die young get through a generation or more in a year. The billions who couldn't take DDT were wasted in a decade, but the billions who could became a species that enjoys DDT for breakfast. Humans are still desperately trying to deal with one decade of the "life-saving" results of DDT, because no one was able to tell them what would happen if they used it. There is no language to describe the future. Language is the past energetically trying to cope with the present, memory trying to cope with decision and action. All the rest is guesswork, however educated. One thinks of the "brightest and best" cooking up Vietnam on their computers. One wants to cry.

Writing makes memory both cumulative and discriminating. It discards, replaces, refines, but it is still language. Language is not reality, nor does it create anything new, however much it rearranges what goes on. It does, on occasion, invent (in the sense of find or discover), but it discovers only what is, whether it is Mars, or the moon, or some unnoticed cranny of the psyche landed on by Allen Ginsberg. I remember an anti-nuclear-testing physicist telling me, "There's no need for testing. I can lie on my bed at night and figure out the results." But, of course, he couldn't. Not all the results of universal distrust, loathing, spiritual nausea, terror can be figured out—all those qualities of the subconscious lay beyond the imperialism of language.

The trouble with intelligence, to the extent that any quality so ephemeral can be measured or quantified, is its kinetic aspect. A physicist at a major university, which has faculty housing as a prerequisite, drove the building and grounds department crazy with his complaints about the floor lamps in his living room. Sometimes they worked and sometimes they didn't, he insisted. An electrician would come over and test all the lamps. They inevitably worked. He would go back to the shop. The next day would come another call and another complaint. Tested again, the lamps would be fine. Finally, the head of the building and grounds paid a visit in the evening when the physicist was at home and the two of them checked out the lamps. When they were all lit, the university's head fix-it man went over to the doorway and checked the wall switch. All the lights went out. The Nobel Laureate was beside himself. "Why didn't you explain this to me when we moved in?" he gasped.

There is no generalization about physicists or other highly intelligent people to be gathered from this story. Another physicist could have solved the problem in a split second. It is just that intelligence is no guarantee of its own kinetic application. It will not necessarily move a person from a failed floor lamp to a wall switch anymore than it helped Einstein to make change or drive a car. Yet some people who score abysmally on IQ tests and fail in school work are capable of complex adaptive behavior. There are high school dropouts in New York City who intuitively understand the welfare system far better than the mayor, although they couldn't possibly explain its structure in words.

If, as Professor Arthur Jensen[2] insists, black people cannot deal with abstractions, it is possibly because for 300 years abstract thought could have gotten them killed. Adaptive behavior in a highly hostile and dangerous social environment requires a kind of particular awareness. One must not miss a trick. One must cope very precisely with the immediate. It is a question of being aware of as much as possible simultaneously and ready to move quickly in response to any small systemic aberration.

Abstract thought, on the other hand, is the luxury of a safe and leisurely environment where privacy is easily accessible. Anyone who ever thought abstractly in combat survived by luck alone. *Abstract*, derived from the Latin, is *drawn away*, unrelated to one's environment, as an "abstracted" person is withdrawn from his environment. What it requires to think abstractly is an aggressive, conscious excision of particulars irrelevant within a paradigm, which is, by definition, exclusive. The peripheral must be utterly neglected. For 300 years any black person enslaved in America who neglected the peripheral or committed himself or herself

2. Arthur R. Jensen, *Environment, Heredity, and Intelligence* (Cambridge, MA: Harvard Educational Review) 1969.

to a paradigm more exclusive than "How do we get through *this* week?," was either extremely brave, or in serious trouble, or both.[3]

One can move from this conjecture to the conclusion that those black people capable of abstract thought were destroyed because quality of mind was maladaptive in their situation, and this left a race bereft of high intelligence. I think that this kind of reasoning sells human intelligence short. I suspect that the same intelligence is applied abstractly or kinetically. It is the quality of the culture within which intelligence is nurtured which determines whether it will apply itself to the abstract or to the kinetic, or determines the balance between the two applications.

The part that Social Darwinism plays in the oppression of black people is far subtler and more effective than the eugenics argument of inferior black intelligence. Most black people find the idea of their intellectual inferiority to whites hilarious. Circumstances have dictated that blacks study white behavior very, very carefully and they are not impressed with white intelligence. They are, however, as impressed as any other American with the idea of survival of the fittest. It was Social Darwinism that made tokenism such an effective device in keeping American blacks an underclass precisely because it is not a conspiracy, but a shared tacit assumption about the nature of reality, shared by both blacks and whites. Success is heavy stuff. Knowing that one has proved one's "fitness" to survive makes one vulnerable to the manipulation of those who have defined what *fitness* is.

Those blacks who played the game strictly according to the rules with superb kinetic intelligence, those blacks who became officers in both World Wars moved from there into civil service, those blacks who got through college on the GI Bill of Rights and worked their way into professions, or the black insurance business or by whatever means into the middle class, those blacks who became well-paid entertainers, or the top athletes of the nation, all found it difficult not to ask the Social Darwinist question, "Why me?" White people were quick to give an answer that confirmed

---

3. While this may seem contradictory to the riggers' intuitive wisdom, the riggers were unsupervised, safe, and followed no schedule. —Ed.

themselves, "Because you're more like *us,* because you're better fit to survive. If *they* were more like you, they wouldn't be inept and poor. In this country everybody has equal access to the top. Look at *you.* Nobody kept *you* from getting to the top." The black middle class knew better. They knew that from their birth, their rise to the top had not quite been like the upward mobility of most whites. It had been more like an obstacle course than a ladder. They had to have been three times more capable at everything than their white competitors. More of everything had been required of them: more energy, more work, more tact, more talent, more patriotism, and more morality. But there was still certain logic to the Social Darwinist argument. They *had* survived; they had, indeed, prevailed over a system loaded against them, a system that they now understood and could make it work *for* them.

They were not only fit to survive, they were a lot more fit to survive than their new white peers. But they had, like most Americans, survived pretty much alone, and certainly not on their own terms. And they had survived, too often, by looking neither to the right nor to the left at the devastation of their black brothers and sisters by the system that they now knew how to make work for them, but for them only as individuals. The key to their continued survival was not to reflect too much, not to talk too much, not to rock the boat, not to get angry or bitter, not to marry interracially. It was not quite the same success. One could, like Richard Wright or Paul Robeson, blow it in a year by simply telling the truth.[4]

I once had the occasion to be in court as a character witness on sentencing day. The sentencing that I was there to

4. Richard Wright (1908–1960) was the author of novels, short stories and poetry that focused on race relations in America. His most notable works were *Uncle Tom's Children* (1938); *Native Son* (1940); *Black Boy* (1945); *The Outsider* (1953); and *White Man, Listen* (1957). Paul Robeson (1898–1976) was a graduate of Rutgers University and the Columbia University School of Law. While famous nationally as a great singer and actor, Robeson also played for the National Football League and was a vocal social activist. He was blacklisted during the McCarthy era for belonging to "subversive organizations." Following the denial of passport privileges, his career plummeted. —Ed.

witness was a long time in coming, but I wasn't bored. The judge was a truly great judge. He addressed every person who came before him as a valuable human being. He was firm, perceptive, quick, but above all, careful to be just.

At one point a black man in his mid-sixties was brought in for sentencing. The clerk read the record of his crime to which he pleaded guilty. As I remember it, it was a case involving a rather strenuous armed robbery. At any rate, it didn't make any sense whatsoever in terms of the thin, frail, rather sensitive-looking older male who confessed to it. When the clerk finished, the judge addressed the older man and said, "Sir, I want to ask you one, very important question and I want you to think carefully about it before you answer. *Did you commit this crime?*" The man's face registered considerable distress and fear. He didn't answer immediately, but then he said, "No, your honor, I didn't." Next the judge asked him, "Did your lawyer tell you that if you plead guilty you would get a shorter term in prison?" "Yes, your honor, he did." "Why did you believe him?" The man looked straight at the judge and said in a strong, angry voice, "Because I didn't have any reason to believe anything else." Then followed a curiously long awkward silence. I suddenly realized that the judge was crying.

From a sermon preached at Christ Church,
Cambridge, MA, September 19, 1974.

The only advice the black middle class had for those who had not come as far as they had was to "be brave, work hard, educate yourselves, be punctual, hold your head high, and never give in to despair." Those who gave the advice knew better, and those to whom it was addressed heard it in dazed disbelief. What these middle-class blacks couldn't reveal was their pain, their rage, their felt sense of their own blackness, their agony of guilt and compassion for the terrible fate of being black in America, and their knowledge that this agony did not disappear with middle-class security. They didn't live as long as white people. The stress of rage turned inward is the greatest cause of psychogenic disease. People die of rage as well as kill. The early civil rights figures to emerge out of this confusion were pioneers in the purest sense of the word. Pioneering is not leadership. It is usually flight. But it is, nevertheless, the beginning of something new. It opens up existence, and, if one is "called out" rather than driven out, as in the case of Moses and Abraham, it begins the generation of "a people." The children (the generations to come) carry the potential for becoming a people. One of these children was Martin Luther King, Jr.

Meeting Martin Luther King

In 1962, I was the director of a Christian farm community in Western Massachusetts. It was what is called an "intentional" community. That is, it was a group of people who, almost fifty years before I became director, had decided to live together; it was led by a charismatic Christian farmer who built a community modeled on the early church. It invited into its common life anyone who needed the support of such a community to get through a difficult period in their lives. When I arrived, there were guests who were just out of mental hospitals, just out of jail, a person blinded by cataracts awaiting an operation, mothers with children who had just been through a difficult divorce, alcoholics, or just people down on their luck. Guests were expected to help with the tasks of community life, to work in the extensive gardens, cut wood, wash dishes, or do whatever was necessary to keep the place going, that they could do.

Among the guests in 1962 was a black Episcopal priest who had been secretary of the Montgomery Improvement Association, Martin Luther King's base community in Alabama. He had, as well, been the rector of a small, poor black parish. He broke under the stress of constant telephone threats to blow up his church and kill his wife and children, the stress of being jailed, the stress of fifteen-hour days being a pastor while organizing demonstrations and helping run the association. His bishop sent him to a private mental hospital on Long Island where he made a quick recovery and came with his wife and children from there to the farm where he soon made his presence felt. There had been some resistance among the members of the community to his coming. He saw that I was under stress enough and never asked me, as director, to deal with racist incidents. He dealt with them one by one as they came up, and remarkably soon he was firmly established in the community. He had worked his way through college and seminary as an upholsterer, and he upholstered all the chairs in the main house. He was a superb pastor and immediately helped me shoulder the pastoral load of the farm, a load that had had me close to my wits' end. . . . His support to me was of inestimable value.

At the same time there was a young woman at the farm after five years in a state mental hospital. Jill was not psychotic, just sort of quiet and fragile. When she spoke she made good sense, but she seldom spoke. She showed no emotion, except sometimes to cry for an hour at a time. Mainly she quietly worked at the housekeeping assigned to her and kept to herself.

One day, after Bob, the priest, had been on the farm three or four months, we read in the *Berkshire Eagle* that Martin Luther King was coming to speak at Williams College. Bob was naturally very excited at the thought of seeing his friend, Martin, again. We called a meeting of the community, and Bob gave a talk on Dr. King and the Southern Christian Leadership Conference, but when the great day arrived, no one wanted to go with us to hear Dr. King except Jill. This woman, who had never expressed any desire to do anything, was urgent and vocal about coming with us. So the three of us drove up to Williamstown.

Dr. King began with a sermon in the Williams Chapel, and I was immediately disappointed. It was what we in the trade call a pure "BS" sermon, very psychological and pastoral about being a whole person, a sermon perfectly put together but bland, never mentioning race or Montgomery or the freedom movement. I could see that Bob was a little let down, too. But Jill was ecstatic. It was, it seemed, addressed just to her.

Dr. King invited us to go down to a conference room for questions and answers. There were, perhaps, a hundred people in the conference room, almost all of them black. But we were not five minutes into the session before it became clear that these were not Americans, but Africans, and they were not a friendly audience. It seemed as if every African student in New England was in that room, and they did not like Dr. King's pacifism. It had no relevance, they said, for the colonial situation in Africa. In a democracy it might work, but even in the United States, they said, it could be no more than an interim tactic, to be used until the whites mobilized to put the movement down violently. It was just a matter of time. What would Dr. King do then? I looked at Bob and I thought I saw him nod his head. It suddenly occurred to me that I might be seeing history made. This group among whom I was sitting might turn out to be a new generation of leaders in their respective countries. What would Dr. King say?

He began by making a careful distinction between pacifism and non-violent direct action, quoting liberally from Gandhi. He reminded them of Gandhi's surprising success during his short stay in South Africa. I could see Dr. King was having an effect. I could see respect grow as the students quit referring to pacifism and began to use the term "non-violent direct action" instead. Questions and statements began to become more specific as each African would talk about his own situation. Dr. King would respond out of his, to me, surprising knowledge of the freedom movement in Africa. He knew a number of African leaders personally. He knew what was going on in country after country. I could see respect grow. The Africans' initial aggressive style disappeared. They began to be almost deferential, asking questions for which they really wanted answers. They had become learners. He had become their teacher. It was not as if he had converted them to non-violence, but they were taking him very, very seriously. Non-violent direct action had become something to consider, a part of the discussion.

When the session was over, Bob took Jill and me up to meet Dr. King. Africans asking even more questions surrounded him. When Dr. King saw Bob he pushed his way through them and embraced him. He asked Bob pointed questions, concerned about how he was doing. Bob introduced Jill and me. We shook hands. And then a surprising thing happened.

Suddenly Dr. King and Jill were engaged in an animated conversation. He asked her a few questions about herself and in a minute she was telling him about her life, about her mental illness, her time spent in the state mental hospital, and her life on the farm. She was completely, vividly alive, responsive, and almost eloquent . . . the conversation went on for ten minutes and I watched his face. It was focused, concentrated, and, above all, full of compassion. Compassion is to fully engage in another's suffering without defense. Finally, he put his hand on her shoulder, smiled and said, "Jill, I hope things will get better for you. It was good to talk with you. God bless you." And he said good-bye to Bob and me and shook hands and walked away.

For the next week or so I was unexplainably happy. Indeed, I was euphoric. I didn't try to examine my euphoria; I just enjoyed it. But I have never been able to leave my own experience well enough alone. As an Episcopalian, I am particularly taken with the Doctrine of the Incarnation, that God became a human being and joined human history, overcame history, and redeemed it with God's Holy Spirit . . . that that love is here to stay and that's enough.

So I began to think about my encounter with Dr. King and I began to realize that he had come into my life as an unexpected gift, a wonderful surprise, and that my strange, pervasive happiness was a real, deep gratitude for his presence in history. What I had hoped for, what I believed in, I suddenly knew was true.

I also learned, or was beginning to learn, that real freedom, the kind that exists in justice and love, is freedom from the rule of fear, particularly the fear of death. Notice, I did not say "freedom from fear," but the "rule of fear." We cannot avoid fear itself, but we can go beyond it, we can refuse to let it dictate what we will do, the choices we will make. But not until we have known the [intersection between] feeling and knowing we call "gratitude." This kind of freedom requires a change of heart, in fact, a grateful heart.

I recall the last time I met Dr. King. It was here in Christ Church. He and Dr. Benjamin Spock[5] were looking for a place to hold a press conference where they would together come out against the war in Vietnam, and we offered the church auditorium. Dr. King was not naïve. He knew what he was doing. Various black leaders had warned him against precisely this. The black historical experience was that the greatest advances in black civil rights had come after wars. The Vietnam War would be no exception. There were many black enlisted men and officers who would be rewarded as patriotic citizens when the war was over. They reasoned there was no connection between civil rights and the war, anyway.

Dr. King explained that that was not what he was about. For him, non-violence was not a tactic or even a strategy; it was absolutely essential to what he believed. He could not face himself as a person of integrity if he was silent about the war while preaching about non-violence . . . I remember a tremor in his hand, sweat on his forehead, and a rich, full, assuring voice, but I knew then, as he knew, and, I suppose everyone in the room knew, this was a face like Christ's, turned toward Jerusalem to be crucified.

Dr. King was among us briefly, like Jesus. He brought us the same saving message that Jesus brought us, the great

5. Benjamin Spock was an American pediatrician and author of an acclaimed handbook on child-rearing, entitled *Baby and Childcare*, published in 1946. The book immediately became the standard reference for a generation of post-World War II parents. He was a lifelong civil liberties advocate and he vehemently opposed the Vietnam War. —Ed.

hope we share with all the people on Earth . . . The war went on, tens of thousands were killed, mainly Vietnamese. Our domestic violence increases from year to year. Sales of small pistols that fit into women's handbags are huge. I could go on with the same old, boring litany of violence we read daily in the newspapers or see directly on television.

People who accept everything they have as what they have coming, or what they have earned by their own merit, must inevitably end up as each other's adversaries. If we have forgotten gratitude, how to give thanks, we have forgotten how to forgive, how to support and console each other, and how to care much about anything except our own survival.

For me Dr. King was, indeed *is*, living proof that there is no other way to understand reality, to understand it as Jesus did, as it issues from a loving God. "Be realistic," the leaders said to Dr. King. But he wasn't realistic; he was real. He was rooted in the reality of the Gospel. He knew and he proved it again, that "love is here to stay, and that's enough."

From an address given at Christ Church,
Cambridge, MA, November 15, 1995.

KING'S LEGACY

King was born into a situation that provided the leisure and safety for abstract thought within a subculture with very fresh memories of what it was like, and what it took, to survive from week to week. He was murdered helping to organize black garbage collectors in Memphis. He was not overly concerned with his own survival or proving his own fitness. Hans Kung quotes J. B. Metz as saying that Christianity is "the activation of 'a dangerous and liberating memory.'"[6] King found this dangerous and liberating memory in

---

6. Kung, *On Being a Christian*, 121. J. B. Metz was a German Roman Catholic theologian who was a proponent of *Political Theology*. He focused on the social, cultural, and economic work of the *polis* in light of the Gospel. —Ed.

himself and found himself capable of activating the same memory in millions of black and white people around the world. It was the opposite of Social Darwinism, insisting that in sacrificial love, not the survival of the fittest, lies the heart of reality. Love, not death, has the ultimate dominion over the human condition.

But King did not immediately swing into action without indulging in some formidable abstract thought. The black dilemma since the Civil War was the despair that came with knowing that, even had their civil rights been enforced, black people were still a racial minority viciously stereotyped as inferior. As a minority, they could exert political power only in a very few localities—and never at a national level, or so it seemed. It was when King's pondering of this dilemma converged with Gandhi's concept of Satyagraha that the alternative of "truth force," or "soul force," emerged to become an alternative both to revolution and to traditional politics. King's non-violent direct action was something new in the West, and King's brilliant global apprehension of the system, his understanding of the interrelationships among economics, government, law, culture, and religion, made him the ideal person to implement it.

King did not begin by organizing the winners. He did not establish a constituency among the black middle class except for those black ministers in whom he activated the dangerous memory of liberation. The first issue, the segregation of an absolutely common public facility—the transportation system of Montgomery, Alabama—was a perfect example of King's sense of *kairos*, his sense of the appropriate time within the inner dynamics of a system. The humiliation and inconvenience of bus segregation were a common experience of *all* blacks. While all bus drivers were white, the bus service was heavily dependent on black use. The black boycott of the bus service was a simple enough act to make the effect economically and politically; it was massive and immediate. There were cars enough in the black community to make it possible, but not without hardship, for all blacks to get to work. Organization was centralized through the churches. Finally, the event was almost immediately significant to get national news coverage. Like the dissolution of a bad marriage, it all began with one woman who simply had had enough.[7] It was something anyone could grasp.

King, then, did not begin with the winners or the losers because he didn't believe in the reality of either category. He began at the beginning. He began with everybody. The goal he sought was a goal that anyone with any self-esteem at all (even if repressed) wants for himself or herself—justice. Justice is also something that everyone has or no one has. This dangerous memory of liberation seems to lie fallow in most people, but it can be activated, and was activated in both blacks and whites. The genius of King was that he understood the relationship between the affirmation and acceptance of the self and the will for justice. He saw that for a person to want to be free, that person has to think of him or herself as worthy of being free.

Studs Terkel told a story, while being interviewed on Public Radio, which points up the issue that King faced. Terkel was interviewing a white working man, taping the interview for one of his books. The man's life was in shambles. His wife had left him. One of his sons was a heroin addict; the other son was in jail. Terkel brought up the war in Vietnam and the man became emotional. "We've got to stick in there! We've got to beat those communists! We've got to win that war!" "Why?" Terkel asked him. "Because we're number one! That's why!" Then Terkel asked him, "Are you

---

7. According to a chronology of the Civil Rights Movement and the Montgomery, AL, bus boycott, Miss Parks was a member of the NAACP and The Montgomery Improvement Association, a black activist movement. Two other women were arrested on buses before Ms. Parks but were not chosen by the Association to challenge their arrest due to their leaders' determination that they could not garner the support of whites. When Rosa was arrested for not yielding her seat to a white man in the black section of the bus, her predecessors are said to have exclaimed, "They've messed with the wrong one now!" Parks was arrested for violating the Laws of Segregation ("Jim Crow"), and she appealed her arrest, challenging the legality of such a bill. The Montgomery bus boycott, resulting from her arrest, lasted 381 days. "Rosa Parks Bus: The Story behind the Bus." *The Henry Ford* (2002), www .thehenryford.org/exhibits/rosaparks/story.asp. —Ed.

number one?" The men hesitated briefly and replied, "Christ no. I'm number nothin.'"[8]

People who are incapable of confirming their own being, who can see no significance in the fact that they exist, are not concerned with justice for themselves or others. The Social Darwinist assumptions underlying American culture create such people in large numbers; people who regard themselves as losers, as number zero.

King, by his application of non-violent direct action to social change, made a theological statement in direct contradiction to prevailing Social Darwinist assumptions about human nature. King insisted that the value of a human being is a given and is, in fact, God-given. It does not derive from a person's intelligence, beauty, strength, accomplishment, social status, or power. Human beings were too precious to be treated with physical aggression, and those who insisted on their rights as human beings, while refusing to treat their oppressors as less than human beings, as objects of violence, found themselves increasingly capable of their own self-affirmation. They came to regard themselves as valued members of a meaningful reality. Those responsible for enforcing the law were permitted to do so without the use of force. At no time were they made to feel that their survival was at stake. They were permitted to act humanely, and on occasion, *did* act humanely. Their value as human beings was confirmed as well. At no point did King present the goal of the struggle as victory over white people. When he said and sang "We Shall Overcome," he was saying and singing about overcoming injustice, hatred, violence, alienation, [about] the structures of evil blacks and whites face *together* in this world. The objective of the Civil Rights Movement for King was not to win, but to be reconciled within a more just social system.

But it became clear to King that that social system could not come about so long as the United States was engaged in the war in Vietnam; it was also clear to him, as it was to other black leaders of that period, that if he publicly opposed the war, his power as a spokesperson for Civil Rights would be radically diminished. And

8. Printed reference: Terkel, *My American Century*, 32. —Ed.

so Martin King made one of the rare ethical judgments by a public figure in our time.

To understand the difficulty of this decision, one must remember again how many middle class blacks had made advances through the armed forces, one of the least racist institutions, particularly during times of war. Black Civil Rights leaders felt ambivalent about Vietnam. Black revolutionaries saw a trained cadre of black guerilla soldiers returning and were delighted. None but Martin King seemed, at that time, to fully understand the brutalization and psychic damage that was the human cost of fighting in that war, fighting an enemy who, as some blacks at that time said, "never called me nigger."

And so, with full knowledge that he would lose much black support, that he would be called "pro-communist," that his position as the most powerful spokesperson for black America would be jeopardized, he called a press conference. Along with Dr. Benjamin Spock, King declared his opposition to the Vietnam War.[9] The punishment was swift and devastating. We now know that even the FBI was conspiring to discredit him. Within a year he was murdered.

One tells the truth because it *is* the truth and not a matter of strategy. King had become convinced that no humane, racially integrated society was possible within the value matrix of Social Darwinist American society. After the march he led through Cicero, Illinois, the only demonstration led by King which caused violence beyond police control, he knew that the "movement" was over, the momentum was gone. The escalating competitive violence of American life had reached a level where non-violent social change of any significance would most probably not take place. There was nothing to be done about that but to tell the truth and to pray for God's deliverance.

9. This speech was made at Christ Church in Cambridge, MA, on April 23, 1967. King and Spock had been denied access to a building at Harvard for this purpose and so the Rev. Murray Kenney and his assistant, the Rev. John H. Snow, extended the invitation to have Drs. King and Spock make their appearance there.—Ed.

The basic issue, at the heart of the matter, had ceased to be racial, or political, or even economic. The heart of the matter was religious, and King responded to it religiously, by telling the truth and praying. His final response was faithful, not strategic. There was a kind of uneasiness about King's strategy among both blacks and whites. People worried that he had been just too Christian to be effective in the long run. Many blacks insisted that non-violence was simply reinforcing the passivity of black culture, and destructive to the black people. At the heart of all alternatives to King's leadership was an obsession with black survival. It was a plausible obsession, and to the secular mind these disagreements were also highly rational. It is very hard for a non-Christian, or, for that matter, a white Christian, to accept King's basic, very New Testament assumption that the poor and the oppressed are the chosen people of God, that "poverty" is normal for a humane life, and that their oppressors are doomed to a catastrophe from which the poor will be spared. Economic poverty was, for King, as for Jesus, a powerful *metaphor* for the appropriate spiritual attitude toward the relationship between a human being, his or her neighbor, and the creation. Although King thoroughly enjoyed the prosperity that was his circumstance in life, it did not have salvific power. He took poverty very seriously, understanding that, in all its ambiguity, there was something to be alleviated to the extent to which it was humanly damaging, yet respected for the transformational power of its truth.

From this Christian, very theological point of view, then, the stereotype of the black as passive was for King simply the potential of the poor and oppressed for the building of a cooperative and reconciling community. As for the assimilation of black culture by the dominant culture of white America, King's understanding of the blacks as "chosen" in their poverty and oppression, deeply acquainted Christian truth through their formidable churches, made it impossible for him to conceive of black Christian culture being assimilated by the disintegrating shambles of white culture which he saw around him in the sixties.

It is pointless to argue about whether King was right or not. The issue here is to describe a model of non-Social-Darwinist behavior, and an historical model at that. Within the Social Darwinist scheme, blacks had been the most blamed victims. It was, the argument went, irrational to claim that they were oppressed. "Look at Ralph Bunche, Marian Anderson, and Jackie Robinson.[10] If blacks couldn't make it into the good life, it was obviously because they weren't up to the task in large numbers. Those who 'had what it takes' were as free to raise their position in life as anyone else," the white public reasoned. King left the rational arguments against such preposterous claims to others. Kenneth B. Clark[11] and the Supreme Court had already invalidated those claims psychologically and legally. Yet nothing in the Supreme Court's decision on school desegregation or even the passage of the Civil Rights Act in 1964 questioned the underlying assumptions of Social Darwinism. Suddenly blacks were free to compete for their piece of the action and they did; suddenly there were a lot of black winners, and for the first time, there was a great number, a disproportionate number, of black losers.

10. Ralph Bunche, Marian Anderson, and Jackie Robinson were major figures in black history for being on the forefront of removing racial barriers in the United States. Bunche, a political scientist and statesman, was the first black to receive the Nobel Peace Prize (1950) for his work in trying to stabilize Arab–Israeli relations. He was also instrumental in the construction and passage of the Universal Declaration of Human Rights at the United Nations. Anderson, a gifted contralto, was the first black to perform (1939) at the New York Metropolitan Opera as well as at the White House. She was denied access to Daughters of the American Revolution's Constitution Hall (1939) but with the intervention of Franklin and Eleanor Roosevelt was later granted access to the Lincoln Memorial where she performed a concert before 75,000 people on Easter day. Robinson was the first black American to play Major League baseball. In 1947 he signed on with the Brooklyn Dodgers to play second base.

11. Kenneth Bancroft Clark, Ph.D. (1914–2005) was an African American psychologist who taught at the City College of New York. He was the author of ten books on the effects of prejudice and racial discrimination on the personality development of black children. He and his wife, Mamie Phipps Clark, Ph.D., developed the doll test (1939) that measured attitudes of children towards dolls of various ethnicities. Their findings influenced many decisions of the Supreme Court, especially *Brown v. The Board of Education* (1954). Clark was a part of the foundation of the Civil Rights Movement. —Ed.

Martin King's belief, that all human accomplishment comes out of one's own understanding of one's significance as a loved member of a human community, lost the edge of its shaping force in the lives of both blacks and whites. And so the poor black today still, in so many cases, inadequately prepared for work by segregated or just poor schools, living during a time of high unemployment in a society which Harvard economist, John Kenneth Galbraith, has called one of public squalor and private affluence, plied with fantasies of this private affluence by television, is defined by the total social ambience as a "loser." When it defined him as a "nigger," he had something or someone to blame. Now he can blame himself. But he can still hate, and hate exists against the winners, black and white.

The black winner is no "nigger" to his or her white peers. The black middle-class person is now just another adversary like anyone else, except that some white peers believe that blacks have the competitive advantage in the legal support of affirmative action, and will be out to prove a black's professional or occupational inadequacy whenever possible. But this is simply one ploy in a game the blacks have chosen to play.

Martin King had had a different vision and, in the acceptable terms of Social Darwinist reality, that vision failed. The legal enforcement of the racial integration of public schools, the Civil Rights Voting Act, affirmative action, all such events are said to be due more to white fear caused by the massive urban riots of the sixties than by the non-violent persuasion of the Civil Rights Movement under King's leadership. His waning leadership and assassination were the result of the country believing in aggressive competition rather than what he had stood for.

Probably nothing points up the pervasiveness of Social Darwinism more than the difficulty this society, both black and white, has had in dealing with the historical figure of Martin Luther King, Jr. He is given a national holiday; institutions are named after him. Most people suspect that there was something special about him, but they disagree about what it was. He was a great black leader, blacks will tell us, but then they will qualify that statement in several ways. Of course, he was a man of his time. Non-violence was a good tactic in the sixties, but it shouldn't be given ideological significance. He didn't understand fully the need for black separatism or sufficiently see the need for blacks to come closer to their African heritage. His vision of an integrated society was very naïve, and his association with the Church and Christianity was too easily taken as an endorsement of one of the principle institutional agents of black oppression, the Church itself. Whites, too, will usually identify King as a great black leader (meaning a leader of blacks) and add that if it hadn't been for him, we probably would have had worse urban rioting than we did. Some of the qualifications are true and others are not. But all these statements and qualifications suggest a certain anxiety, a feeling that, somehow, a national hero should have been more successful. The anxiety is well founded.

By no standard of current American culture was Martin Luther King, Jr. a success. Although our schools and work and social life are more racially integrated, probably, to some degree, as a result of King's efforts, our institutional life is disintegrating on so many other levels that the achievement may be as spiritually destructive to blacks as segregation. In the end, King believed that racial integration without a religiously based social integration was not possible. So long as both blacks and whites accept social Darwinism as reality, the whole climate of their shared life will be disintegrative rather than integrative, and the killing of the losers will go on, and a disproportionate number will be black. An economy that has managed to have high inflation accompanied by high unemployment is an economy designed to raise competition at every level of society.

The essence of martyrdom is that it witnesses to a more profound, more significant, reality than the culture within which it takes place recognizes. Martin King was both like and unlike other Americans. An anecdote may show this similarity and this difference.

When Medgar Evers, the NAACP representative in Jackson, Mississippi, was murdered, the NAACP thought that the occasion of his funeral should be given national significance. Invitations were sent to prominent blacks and whites and to the leaders of all the civil rights organizations of the time. The seating was carefully planned. On a stage at one end of a college gymnasium were seated the NAACP leadership and the local NAACP leaders, all ministers, who were to conduct the funeral. Martin King and Ralph Abernathy[12] were seated with ten white ministers (the only whites at the funeral) close to the front of the congregation, but certainly not in seats of honor. It was a mild put-down. There were perhaps 5,000 people present.

The funeral began with a series of eulogies that soon turned into exhortations to violence. Radicals from several northern industrial cities had taken over the stage. The gist of their message was that blacks had been non-violent long enough and the time had come for them to leave this building and turn Jackson, Mississippi, into one great pool of blood. King turned to Abernathy and said, " I've got to get onto that stage, Ralph. This is turning into a disaster." Abernathy put his hand on King's shoulder, "Martin," he said, "you are not God. You know that this is NAACP territory. Those ministers up there are good men. They can handle it." King leaned back in his chair, "You're right, Ralph. They can handle it," he replied.

Gently, but decisively, the ministers cut off their eulogies and moved into the powerful, dignified, moving forms of a black Christian funeral service. The rage dissipated, the grief surfaced, and the danger passed. King and Abernathy marched unobtrusively positioned, in the funeral procession. With help from a friend, King could be reminded what the movement was about: a cooperative movement for racial justice of King's SCLC and the NAACP. It was not about competition for turf. King was intensely aware of his own mortality and was one of those rare persons who accepted it

12. Ralph Abernathy (1926–1990), a Baptist minister was considered Martin King's closest friend. Together, they founded the Montgomery Improvement Association (1954) that launched the Montgomery bus boycott and the Southern Christian Leadership Association (1957) that was instrumental in the American Civil Rights movement. Abernathy succeeded King upon King's assassination in Memphis. —Ed.

as a normal part of life, indeed as life's fulfillment. He understood that neither he, nor the human race, nor the planet would survive in the long run. He believed in a life beyond survival and that, in the short run, nothing so degrades human personality as clawing for survival at the expense of others.

The new Social Darwinism agrees to manipulate the social and economic environment enough to provide greater numbers of competitive blacks, largely because a massive black revolt (as seemed possible in the sixties) would both appear maladaptive, as well as not contribute to the survival of the nation. In many cases, the result has actually been a reduction in racism. The question is whether a society which pits man against man, man against woman, woman against man, woman against woman, adult against child, child against adult and, no doubt soon, age against youth and youth against age—whether such a society is superior to one which pits black against white. The question, as Martin King knew so well, was whether we want to live in a society that places humans directly at odds with each other at all.

Racism means a deep, intense, pathological distrust of people of one race for another. But I think it is something more subtle and insidious than that. It has to do with culture and the long love affair of Northern Europeans with genetic biology. Even before the science of genetics was born, the Northern European was obsessed with breeding, with the breeding and cross-breeding of animals and plants and, among the aristocracy, with the breeding of blood lines of the ruling class. Even when I was a kid, I would hear and understand the reference to people with particularly good manners as "well bred"—a curious phrase suggesting a strong belief in the genetic base of complex human behavior.

Of all the stereotypes of black inferiority, the last one to die, and one that is far from dead in this country, or in any of the Northern European nations, is the stereotype of black intelligence as genetically inferior. The attacks on affirmative action, welfare, and job training programs, Washington insists, are not generated by any hatred for black people, or any prejudice: it is an experiment, as is the whole of American culture. The cost of freedom is risk. In a free society, we do not live by an ethic of need; we live by an ethic of merit. It was this ethic that brought about the highest standard of living in the world. It is this ethic that is the American way of life. This way of life is open to anyone who possesses aggressive intelligence and the will to apply it. The enemy is ourselves and the insane illogic of our ideology. So long as we are captive, we shall find it very difficult to love at all, least of all to love the God who loves us.

From a sermon preached at Christ Church,
Cambridge, MA, June 16, 1986.

Christian choices lead us to a moment where, if we run away from it, we have betrayed our faith. Martin King was not an impulsive person, and he was not a demagogue. He began by explaining that his was a personal and private statement. As a Christian he was opposed to violence at every level: in the civil rights movement, in the peace movement, and in foreign policy and international affairs. I don't think he said more than that.

I have been close to Martin King under stress before. He was never the nerveless, totally tranquil saint he was often made out to be; but this time the strain, the agony was very noticeable. And so when the issue of the war came along, he was put to the ultimate test as to whether he would "show forth in his life what he professed by his faith." Ironically, by opposing the war, Martin King reduced his credibility as a non-violent leader.

No one knows what the course of events might have been had he kept silent; Martin King was soon dead. What followed was *our* history, not *his*. He did what he chose to do. In a world of electronic surveillance, computerized warfare, nuclear bombs, and all the rest, I saw one human being act in total faith that Jesus was God. I saw one person refuse to play the odds, refuse to calculate, refuse to be a winner, refuse to guarantee his own success. He knowingly chose martyrdom, witnessing to his Lord, over his own happiness or survival.

The purpose of martyrdom is to discover reality, to define truth, and to reveal God. It has no other function. It is not heroism, not a brave and sacrificial act to further a cause. Martyrdom doesn't do good; it defines and reveals the source of good and makes it possible for other humans in their freedom to choose or reject not the good, but God, the dynamic, personal center from whom all good comes.

From a sermon remembering Dr. Martin Luther King's Opposition to the War in Vietnam, preached at Christ Church, Cambridge, MA, April 25, 1976.

4

Social Darwinism and the Institution of Marriage

Fear is always the result of seeing the other, whether it is a person, or a group, or a nation, or even nature itself, as our adversary. In a society that cultivates competition, fear simply becomes the emotional climate within which people live; fear and fear's inevitable result, distrust.

The opposite of fear is faith. Faith is understood as trust, a sort of general sense of the basic trustworthiness of our life together on this planet surrounded by the inclusive love of God. In myself, I have found this kind of faith, this kind of trust, to be uncertain, sometimes strong, sometimes weak and tentative, sometimes non-existent. When I am strong, I am least fearful, I can hear what other people say, I can change my mind, I can handle frustration and learn from it, I can enjoy the presence of people quite unlike myself. But when my faith is weak or vanishes entirely, I find myself getting very focused, very goal oriented, very much concerned with my own achievement and not much aware of other people, except to the extent that they are useful to

65

me in what I want to achieve. I am not consciously fearful, just very concentrated.

As we move forward in time, we do so in a climate of fear and uncertainty about what the future holds. I know that this fear in me will virtually create the circumstances that I fear most unless my faith is sufficient to temper it and leave me free to be aware of other people and willing to cooperate with them. For me this renewal will be found in Jesus Christ, and Jesus Christ will be found in the very midst of those things that I fear most if I dare to address them with a trusting heart.

From a sermon preached at Christ Church,
Cambridge, MA, March 1, 1981.

REDEFINING RELATIONSHIPS

Several years ago I wrote a book on marriage and was then considered expert enough in that matter to be invited to speak around the country, usually to church groups. I discovered that some of those who attended evening meetings arrived well fortified and didn't make much sense during question periods. At least twice full-scale inter-spousal warfare erupted amidst a parish hall full of people. I discovered also that a talk that evoked rational discussion in Massachusetts could cause a near riot in Wisconsin and put people to sleep in California. Regional differences in attitude towards marriage are very real, and, for the most part, attitudes toward marriage still determine attitudes toward the whole matter of human sexuality.

There are, however, in many cities and some suburbs an increasing number of people for whom marriage is not part of the sexual equation at all. They are not "single" in the classical sense, but allergic to contracts. There are also increasing numbers of singles, divorced people, and never-marrieds who would attend my lectures and fly into rages during the question period at a church that organized its educational offerings and parish life in general around the institution of marriage, ignoring what was in some parishes becoming close to a majority of single members.

Since it was impossible to anticipate regional or local issues in the matter of marriage, I decided that a visiting "expert" was of less than no use and quit, rather discouraged with the institution of marriage, and also confused by it. The good turnout at lectures by an unknown person with not very impressive credentials, as well as the high emotional content of questions and comments during the discussion periods, suggested that people were finding marriage difficult and were looking for any help they could get. Yet it was clear that people in different parts of the country were finding different things difficult. It was hard to find any common denominator of suffering. Yet suffering there was in abundance, especially—indeed, primarily—among women, and it manifested itself as fear and anger. Curiously, the woman who passionately defended traditional marriage and family life exhibited the same anger as the divorced woman who claimed that traditional marriage was destructive to women and should be abolished. Both gave the impression that they were fighting for their lives. In fact, the one constant that remains in my memory from those difficult days is a strange image of people, men also, to the extent that they dared speak at all, fighting for their lives.

In some cases, women were fighting men; in others, they were fighting change; in others, they were fighting lifestyle, such as "swinging" neighbors; in others, they were fighting the imperialism of marriage as an institution, the judgmental moralism of bourgeois marriage and family life. Men in some places were still fighting the idea of the working wife and what they saw as the inevitable neglect of children; in other places, they were fighting the inequities of affirmative action legislation which gave jobs to young unskilled women, which men so desperately needed during an economic slump. Or they were fighting what they regarded as the wives of well-paid men working during a time of high unemployment. In this latter case, one suspected the men were talking about their own wives. The only link between one perception of the enemy and another was the level of anger (or fear) that seemed constant in all cases.

At the heart of our problem is the fact that we do not think that we "measure up." We base our self-esteem on performance. We are assaulted by advertising in the mass media that tells us so. We are told that there is something lacking in our social status, or our appearance, or our virility, or our femininity, or our recreational patterns, or our child rearing, or a thousand other things. These are best remedied by spending money on this or that, and when or if we spent the money, we discover that we have to measure up to something new. We should be crazy not to feel this way. The fear and confusion that we feel is the God given signal of our personal survival system, they are not signs of our lack of worth.

What should we do? Aside from those psychologically lucky enough not to buy into these criticisms, we have no answer apart from religion. We have no recourse whatsoever except to assume a faith assumption. We must resort to the absurd. We must base our lives on the assumption held by Martin Luther King, Robert Kennedy, or Mayor Lindsay, that we and everyone born into this world, has value, can love, can build, can create, can learn, and is capable of so much more than the greed and narrowness which our society mostly seems to expect of us.

From a sermon preached at Christ Church,
Cambridge, MA, June 16, 1969.

It seemed appropriate to conjecture on why these women were experiencing their sexual role, whatever that sexual role *was*, at such a high level of fear and anger. And one can *only* conjecture, and many people have. Some have conjectured that the fear and anger are a consequence of women's sudden suspicion that they have been exploited, raped, cheated, used, intimidated, dominated, brutalized, and subjugated by men. Those who conjecture along these lines are, again obviously, women, and they will confess their own fear of men and a "man's world" while demanding a part in it. Others say this anger and fear is, among married women with children, a reaction to that wing of the women's movement that they perceive as vilifying or ridiculing the one thing they know how to do well, which is to be a wife and mother. Whatever cause is assigned to this fear and anger, there seems to be no argument that there is good reason for them on the part of many women and men. Perhaps one more conjecture is in order.

It would seem to me that the effective marketing of birth control and the availability of relatively safe abortions might have been the most radical technological occurrence since the wheel. The acceptance of these phenomena is one of those great mysteries. As usual, the only significant community to see the overwhelming importance of this event was the Roman Catholic Church, but as usual, the Roman Catholic response was dogmatic, unreflective, and less than helpful.[1] Not much time was given to the question, "What can we expect as a result of the use of birth control and abortion, and how can we adapt to their use with minimal chaos and dehumanization?" A great deal of time was devoted to explaining why they shouldn't be used at all. Liberal Protestant thought mumbled something about the ethical responsibility of Christians to plan families, but hardly went beyond that.

It seems to have occurred to very few people that the primary function of the human species from a scientific point of view (middle-class Americans *have* a specific point of view) is the reproduction of itself, and that this new medical technology had just rendered that primary function more difficult. It was not that something so elemental should not be tampered with (although that may perhaps be what we learn), it is that it should not be tampered with unreflectively and for profit. The typical American

1. On December 31, 1930, the Roman Catholic Church banned any artificial means of birth control including condoms, diaphragms, cervical caps, and spermicides because they interrupted normal and natural functions in the creation of life. On July 28, 1968, after an eight-year study, Pope Paul VI, in *Of Human Life*, issued a decree that affirmed the traditional teaching of the Church declaring the use of all contraceptives a "mortal sin."—Ed.

reaction to the accessibility of birth control was to go buy some. It was about that reflective. Middlemen doctors concerned themselves with possible side effects or keeping the stuff away from minors (for a while).

Let us consider, now that we have some hindsight, what actually happened. In the past, human societies have been organized around reproduction and child rearing to the extent that they have been adaptive. The long gestation period, the often longer nursing stage, and then the extraordinarily long dependent childhood of humans had to be dealt with one way or another by the way society was organized. If one considers, for instance, the early days of the Industrial Revolution, one sees a sudden maladaptive economic change that didn't allow for the peculiarities of human reproduction and child rearing. Granted the normal slowness of social change once a certain practice is assimilated, one cannot help but notice how quickly public outrage and the organization of labor took women and children out of the labor market and placed them back in the home and then arranged for men to make enough money to maintain them there. Either this happened or a revolution rearranged society so that at least children were cared for, and women were given an option whether they should work or not.

The point here was the near inevitability of pregnancy within marriage. Equal access to each other's body was a part of the marriage contract but interpreted differently by each sex.

APPLYING BATESON'S RELATIONSHIP ANALYSIS

The complementary nature of marriage, with its dominant-submissive character, was not a male chauvinistic conspiracy, but a necessary arrangement for rearing an indeterminate number of children in a world where, until 1940, technology was crude and the maintenance of life was physically demanding for all but the rich.

The anthropologist Gregory Bateson divides all human relationships into two categories, complementary and symmetrical.[2] Complementary relationships assume a hierarchical structure to society that begins with parent–child and moves on to teacher–student, manager–worker, officer–enlisted personnel, and all other subtle ranking variations in a complex society with a high degree of specialization. Marriage was traditionally such a complementary relationship. Bateson points out that the danger of such a relationship is the slow or sudden intensification of its inner dynamic so that the dominant partner becomes increasingly dominating and the other submits more and more. The result of this intensification, unchecked, is the destruction or revolt of the submissive partner. Bateson uses the example of colonialism at its worst.

The symmetrical relationship, in contrast, is between equals and is often a working relationship, as found in a team, or group, or cooperative enterprise. Its danger is a kind of competitive escalation that, unchecked, results in a split or perhaps bloody combat, even death. Bateson uses as an example the arms race between the United States and Russia.

In any viable society, both relationships take place in a rulebound social matrix with many checks to keep them from going haywire. In society at its most stable, complementary marriage has many customary implicit rules for supporting and maintaining its humaneness. An abusive husband is ostracized; an overly submissive wife is ridiculed. The kind responsible husband who is a "good provider," who disciplines his children firmly and good naturedly, who is faithful and attentive to his wife's needs, is accorded the respect and affection of the community. The "good wife and mother," is accorded the same respect and affection from the community. The marriage itself exists in a climate of confirmation and support. The model for such a marriage is clearly defined, but there are many rich variations within its complementarity, and such variations are socially acceptable so long as the basic complementarity remains.

2. Bateson, *Steps to an Ecology of the Mind*, 324.

Effective birth control and safe abortion would alter the complementary structure of marriage and make it symmetrical. With the passing of the indeterminacy of family size came an extraordinary number of alternatives for structuring marriage, but the particular moment in American history at which these new reproduction options entered society determined that the structure would be basically symmetrical.

The social function of sexual morality was to protect the vulnerability of women who had no way of managing their fertility except by sexual abstinence. Adultery was immoral for men not only because of the pain it brought to the marital relationship, but also because of the extreme social turbulence caused by extramarital pregnancy and the stigma attached to illegitimacy.

When the Victorians said that a promiscuous man had "ruined" a woman, they used the word "ruined" accurately. The promiscuous or impulsive woman who found herself pregnant was faced with only dreadful options. Effective birth control and safe, legal abortions largely removed this vulnerability in women, and sexual morality ceased to have such a clear social function. Men no longer needed to "protect" women (presumably from the men themselves), and the need for complementarity in all relationships between men and women was no longer obvious.

But the complementary marriage had fallen on difficult days even before the perfection of birth control, again, as a consequence of improved technology. The sixties saw the explosion of motor vehicles, super highways, and air travel that resulted in a level of transiency unparalleled in human history, and with this transiency came a new anonymity and the failure of community. Improved domestic technology also made it possible to accomplish as much household maintenance in an hour as had taken twelve hours a decade earlier. This left the children as the wife's primary responsibility, but she was too often forced to meet this responsibility in a suburb where what relationships she could foster tended to be competitive, transient, harried, and careless. The anonymity of children in a transient community made the free play of children more risky than had been the case in stable neighborhoods where all adults and children knew one another by name and most adults took responsibility for the discipline and safety of neighborhood children.

The lives of children became highly organized, and this organization was up to the parents, mainly the mothers. It was both time-consuming and, for the most part, boring. Another aspect of transiency and anonymity was the absence of community reinforcement of the mother's complementary role. Husbands away at work were not around to appreciate domestic and parental expertise. In these suburbs, supportive respect and affection engendered by social competitiveness often turned into envy. The energy and thoughtfulness required to raise children during this time of rapid change accompanied by a great deal of moving about was more than most people bargained for.

Family is a bold, complex, rich, and powerful metaphor for what the world is like, which has as its dynamic center parental love. It is a universal metaphor. All humans, even the most neglected and wretched of the earth, know what family is, if only through the pain of its absence or its distortion into something evil. God intends history to be a home for human beings. In the person of Jesus, God lived and died in the world as a human being to transform history into a home.

At the heart of parental love is sacrifice, a giving, a committing of oneself to make the family whole and healthy. This involves suffering, self-diminishment, the curbing of appetite and desire, the limiting of private goals and, if necessary, taking on death itself. Parental love is sacrificial love, but its power is in its vulnerability. It is this power which puts the world at risk. Remove the divine and universal significance of parenthood and the family loses its hospitality, its generosity, its inclusiveness, its welcome, and becomes an entirely self-centered force in the human community. Either that, or it simply falls apart into aimless decadence and becomes a heap of lonely, desperate individuals, each trying to survive on its own. The worst is a corruption of the best.

From a sermon preached at Christ Church,
Cambridge, MA, March 15, 1987.

From what I've observed, a family often reached some sort of critical mass and exploded with the adolescence of the first child. Divorce came thick and fast. The woman, who had been the submissive one in the complementary marriage, revolted. The relationship became symmetrical, and since there were no rules for a symmetrical marriage, no customary limits to keep competition from escalating, the split came, often after some ugly warfare.

Baby boomers confess to vivid memories of their parents suffering and to having thought at that time, "If this is what marriage and family life—if this is what it is to be an adult—I want no part of it." The great unanswered question about children was, simply, "What to do with them?" This thought contributed to the generation gap of the sixties and to a very low self-image for those young people as they moved beyond adolescence.

The reasons for the low self-image are complex and have to do with our "technopathic" society. The place of children was in a state of limbo. Work for children, "chores," was largely busy work. Children were seldom regarded as helpful. There was no way that they could make their helpfulness measure up to the level of needfulness, and they were intensely aware of this. Having graduated from Little League, Scouts, music lessons, ballet, and so on, they made few contributions to family life and tended to "hang around" or watch television. In fact, all a child could do, if he or she wanted to please his or her parents, was to excel. If the child proved to be a winner, they received praise, but praise itself is a kind of psychic distancing operation. It is unilateral and can be withdrawn at any time.

The adolescents of the sixties and the seventies were faced with the broad acceptance of the pill, the legalization of abortion, the Vietnam War, the pressure to get into college, and the sudden universal consciousness of what is often called the "global crisis"—the convergence of overpopulation, pollution, world hunger, and the diminishment of energy resources. It was a mixed-up time. The non-winners wondered what use they were to anyone. If the boys didn't get into college they would probably get drafted and sent to Vietnam. If the girls didn't get into college, the boys they might normally have married would have been drafted. They could get jobs, but most of the jobs paid badly. Marriage itself was an appalling thought to many of them, but what was truly disastrous was the runaway competitiveness that pervaded every aspect of these peoples' educations and home lives. Even in their escape, the flower child ambience of the middle and late sixties became permeated with precisely the same competitiveness that informed all the others. The Woodstock Nation was competitive in its own bizarre ways.

It was into this "compete or perish" environment that the changing male-female relationship evolved: shifting from complementary to symmetrical relationships, from the support and approval of the small community to a transient society without rules, limits or tradition. Since a part of this "symmetricality" involved affirmative action for women in the workplace, women's experience of men increasingly in competitive work situations where women learned to compete or perish (or, like the men, to think that they must learn to compete or perish). Their work life, then, provides few guidelines for how symmetrical or even sexual relationships might be maintained without the marital relationship. As many of these couples entered their thirties, they became involved in a sexual ranking game with less and less feeling and more and more isolation until they finally complained that nothing made any sense at all. "I don't feel anything," they'd say to their psychiatrist, or social worker, or marriage counselor, or minister. "I feel dead inside. Everything outside of me seems unreal; I can't sustain a relationship. I can't love. I can't be close to anyone." And so it goes, and the more astute counselor knows that this kind of narcissism will quite often not respond to treatment. Therapy with such a person can, at any moment, become a complex, highly competitive game, with the patient charming, seducing, intimidating, manipulating, and engaged in a life-and-death battle to avoid even an honest assessment of his or her behavior, to say nothing of going any deeper. Others seek no help and move instead into alcoholism or suicide. Others still develop into consummate gamesmen, hardly seeming to notice their own blighted humanity, suffering hardly at all as they cause suffering to anyone who gets too close.

Much thought has gone into what is described here, and clergy have received no little criticism for the lack of depth or a flat refusal to marry couples who obviously have no intention of taking the institution of marriage seriously. This all would be very well, but those marriages that seem, by present cultural standards, to be made in heaven, are in most jeopardy. Those human values most honored are precisely those values that are destructive to a marriage. Winners tend to marry winners; marriage today is "for as long as we both shall . . . win? Succeed? Survive?" Expressed sarcastically, within a marriage there must be "growth" on the part of individuals, not maturity or diminishment. And death is *certainly* for losers. Everyone knows that winners keep their options open, and marriage, like having children or dying, seems like a massive closing off of alternatives, a quick way to lose.

Now, these are very serious questions. At first glance, not to have children at all seems like a hedonistic decision based on self-interest. Since the beginning of time, in the North Temperate Zone women have been considered, and have learned to consider themselves, significant *primarily* in terms of bearing and raising children. We do not know what family life would be like, or whether it would be possible, where the ideal, the model, was the optimal development of each family member rather than the traditional ideal for the institution (and the organic reality) of family itself. It is a logical and probably human impossibility that a highly competitive symmetrical relationship will endure for very long or even come to a graceful end. In a society where all but the very rare symmetrical relationships do tend to be competitive, it is hard to conceive of symmetrical marriage creating a family that took its own corporate life seriously. Men and women in competition with each other may very well create ultimate social chaos, but this does not mean that their relationship must be complementary. The great challenge to human sexuality is to develop a social matrix within which symmetrical relationships become customarily co-operative, and effective social limits are put on competition where it is clearly maladaptive.

We move a lot. We often "succeed." We surpass the achieve-ments of our parents. We "outgrow" our communities of birth and childhood. We become more mobile—upwardly and laterally. We break one attachment after another. But we don't grieve. Instead, we grow nostalgic, sentimental, and reactionary. We mumble about a return to the "basics." Or we adapt to life as pure process, and find what satisfac-tion we can in pure technique, in what is called today as the "pursuit of excellence." The nostalgia, the "back to basics," is often a good inclination gone wrong. It reflects the nor-mal human desire to address and be addressed by the Holy. For individuals, as for the culture of which they are a part, the loss of one's narrative, the cumulative discontinuities in one's story, needs to be grieved.

Snow, *The Impossible Vocation*, 68.

5

The Language of Institutional Life

A week ago I heard the medical advisor to our president's campaign being asked why neither he nor his opponent had not done more than merely mention AIDS in their campaigns.[1] He replied, "You see, they can't. If they got into AIDS, they would get into sex, they would get into drugs, they would get into poverty, they would get into race. If they get into any of these things, they would make themselves vulnerable." In other words, if they get into any aspect of the suffering of the world, they make themselves vulnerable. These may be the truest words uttered in the entire campaign.

Jesus could have told him that. Any movement toward the suffering of the world may result in terrible wounds. Better to talk about making America competitive again. Better to declare a war on drugs than to ask why people turn to drugs. Better to declare a war on cancer than to ask what we're doing to the environment to cause cancer. Better to declare a war on AIDS rather than ask why so many of

1. George H. W. Bush vs. Michael Dukakis.

79

the poor regard AIDS as just one more thing. Better to declare a war on homelessness rather than to build low-cost housing or sheltered treatment for the chronically mentally ill. The minute any politician turns toward the suffering of the world, his opponent shouts, "Look at him! He's a pessimist, a doomsayer, a bleeding heart." And too many of the American people turn to pro-football or *Dallas*,[2] where the fit survive and no one has to worry about the losers, about the suffering of the world.

From a sermon preached at Christ Church,
Cambridge, MA, November 6, 1988.

THE ISSUE OF COMMUNICATION

The new Social Darwinism is not a coherent, explicit social philosophy—at least, not yet. It is hard for us to think in any disciplined, scientific way about the future of humanity in other than evolutionary terms, and even where, as in the case of socio-biologist E. O. Wilson, altruism is regarded as one dimension of adaptive behavior, the blessing of competition as a benign shaping force in history is a great temptation. Perhaps *benign* is one word too many. Competition is simply a shaping force, or perhaps the primary shaping force. That it is a shaping force can't be denied. That it is *the* shaping force must certainly be considered.

French philosopher and Jesuit priest Pierre Teilhard de Chardin mentions the massive wastefulness of the evolutionary process; how vast are the sheer numbers of creatures made suddenly or slowly maladaptive and then extinct by climate change or other unlikely interventions into the cosmic system.[3] Perhaps it was de Chardin's experience with modern warfare that made him think of this wastefulness. As a stretcher-bearer in World War I, he was

2. Produced by Warner Brothers, this popular evening television serial (1978–1991) was based on the lives of a fictional wealthy Texas family. —Ed.

3. de Chardin, *The Phenomenon of Man*, 134.

part of the grimy insectoids slaughtering for turf, the anonymous hordes of soldiers in uniform hurling themselves upon each other's fire year after year until the death toll ran into the millions. Freud said something to the effect that no other biological theory is so tempting to apply to social behavior as Darwin's.

Teilhard was often so tempted, sometimes with considerable wit. At one point he comments that people observing the planet Earth from outer space between 1890 and 1940 might have concluded that a radical mutation had taken place in *homo sapiens* resulting in the development of a carapace. He was referring to the extraordinarily swift growth of automotive technology, and added that the automobile followed exactly the pattern of a newly evolved phylum. In terms of evolutionary time, almost overnight in biological evolution there will be hundreds of variations on a newly evolved phylum, but as the phylum gets older natural selection reduces the variations to a few basic models. So it was with the automobile. Within fifteen years of its invention there were hundreds of different makes and models, but the natural selection of the market place soon reduced the number to a handful, all very similar in design and engineering.

But one could carry Teilhard's fantasy much further. The observer in outer space might have noticed that with the development of the carapace came a revolution in the total organization of human society involving elaborate highway systems, suburbs ringing the cities (cities which were themselves often obscured with smog), an extraordinary transiency and mobility of the newly carapaced humans, and the curious ritualized mating of these creatures with what appeared to be a machine and was, in fact, a gas pump.

And so it goes. But it is intriguing that humans in large numbers seem to behave most like social insects, seem to be most genetically programmed, when they are most *mindlessly obedient* to their own technology. There was no conscious choice made to develop the internal combustion engine as a basic mode for propelling human transportation. This massive change in human behavior was pure drift: no votes, no cost–benefit studies, just utter heedlessness, pure impulsivity. Yet there was an almost unquestioning assent to its rightness. Even as late as 1970 I met a young man with a fresh doctorate in geology who had written his thesis on fossil fuels and who was about to leave for Alaska. I asked him about oil. "Our supply of oil is inexhaustible," he replied. "There are only the technical problems of finding it and getting it out of the ground." So much for the objectivity of the expert faced with genetic technological drift. Even I know that finite substances are not inexhaustible, but to him that smelled of theology.

The question is, where do we get all of these bad, maladaptive, self-destructive ideas such as the infinitude of fossil fuels? Clearly, no one sat down and lectured Americans on how the automobile was the most appropriate mode of transportation for Lockean-Social Darwinists. No one explained to us that our transportation should be as individuated, and private and competitive as the rest of our lives. Somehow, we send each other messages that tell us what we are supposed to do and to be, and this process clearly goes beyond what we are consciously taught by schools and parents. Those things we learn to believe in our bones, the deepest value assumptions which give a degree of pattern to our decisions and keep our lives from being purely random and impulse ridden, are things we learn from the customary way the institutions we are a part of go about their business. In a healthy society the explicit, consciously expressed purposes of our institutional life are consonant with the customary decisions and actions of our institutions. Word and deed have a certain consonance, as with a healthy person, both word *and* deeds send messages.

According to communications theory every message has two parts, report and command. The report part is simply the information that the message conveys, while the command part tells what to do with the information and defines the relationship between the person sending the message and its recipient. "John Smith resigned from his position as Vice President of Jones and Jones on January 23." "You're not going to like this, boss, but Smith quit on us yesterday." The basic information of these two sentences is roughly the same, but they say very different things about relationships. The relationship aspect of a message is called meta-communication. In interpersonal relationships it can be quite complex and thoroughly unclear, but very often it is the most important part of the message. It involves the choice of words and grammar, the volume and nuance of tone in speaking, facial expression, and body language. Indeed, it involves the whole person communicating, consciously and unconsciously.

COMMUNICATION AND ROLE

Institutions meta-communicate as well, and the meta-communication of institutions is even more complex and more easily misunderstood than that of persons. The family, for instance, is an institution, probably the most basic one. So are science, law, business, industry, medicine, education, the penal system, government, the media, etc.

In family therapy one discovers that the family as a group will often expect a certain kind of behavior from individual members. It will, so to speak, assign roles—the achiever, the slow one, the dreamer, the comic, even the bad one, even, alas, the rotten one. The family will, somehow, manage to reinforce behavior that fits the assigned role and ignore (or punish) behavior that does not fit their expectations. All this, sometimes, is quite apart from the assumptions of sex role behavior. In other words, there is a kind of group meta-communication going on which can have a cumulative effect on shaping the character of the individual. It seems that the equilibrium, the smooth running of the family system, depends on having these roles consistently maintained.

If one becomes a doctor, one will discover, even as a pre-med undergraduate, that the institution of medicine has a number of expectations about what kind of person one will be. Unlike families, it is not a special but a general role. Until recently, this set of expectations included one's politics, how one should feel (or not feel), one's economics, one's sexuality, one's religion (one should be an atheist or agnostic), etc. All this is quite apart from the explicit expectations of dedication, intelligence, skill, professionalism, and human compassion.

Medicine, however, is no different from other institutions. The teacher, the school principal, the college professor, the minister, the industrial manager, the vice president of marketing, the lawyer, each has an institutional persona thrust upon him or her, and to the extent that this role is rejected, the individualist will be institutionally ignored or punished. Yet the role is seldom explicitly taught. These outsiders are often people who have a great deal of trouble understanding what institutions and other people are meta-communicating to them. Many of them are, quite literally, literal minded. They understand and accept the information presented to them in words, but they are often confused by the implicit message about relationships that exist to some degree in all messages. They are people who can't cope with the institutional double bind where the institution's explicit message is often directly contradicted by its meta-communication.

Until recently, the assumption of medical school was precisely the same as that of academic science. An individual's intellectual gifts are his own marketable private property. Thus a highly competitive academic climate was deliberately encouraged. Heavy work loads, a strict marking system, and a curious kind of academic hazing (making physics compulsory for someone whose goal is to become a psychiatrist) were the norm, and "cheating" was met with immediate dismissal. The trouble is that all of this competition is utterly inappropriate to the actual practice of medicine. In some circles the pedagogical style was altered to create a more cooperative approach to learning medicine. In others it wasn't, and students simply began to cheat.

The cheating (and this was true throughout the entire academic enterprise) began as an ideological exercise, a kind of revolutionary rip-off of a repressive reactionary system, but it became a part of the total competitive process. The task for all but the most brilliant demands a cooperative institutional style, but the cheater is made to feel like a shrewd entrepreneur by the school's refusal to bless cooperation over competition. The answer is an *almost* explicit commitment to Social Darwinism, an honest belief that competition generates a higher motivation to learn. It is not surprising that the current public image of the physician is becoming one of an entrepreneur selling his skills to the highest bidder. This would be fine with most Americans except that without access to these skills the public would suffer or die. This puts the doctor–patient relationship into a category too much like the dealer–heroin-addict category. A very high ambivalence factor here is no doubt responsible for malpractice suits in such abundance. Interestingly, both doctor and patient are coming to see their relationship as an adversarial one. This unfortunate occurrence is the result of institutional meta-communication. The medical schools are not consciously trying to turn out business entrepreneurs. The doctors are not trying to create an adversarial relationship with their patients. But there are meta-communicational messages flying all over the institution of medicine that this is how things ought to be.

It is hard to make sense out of an existence where human agency has become so remote, where so much of our corporate life has been entrusted to massive technological systems, designed and built by humans, certainly, but apparently becoming more autonomous every day.[4] It is hard to make sense out of a world where blame cannot be laid, and even harder to live in a world where everyone seems to be blaming everyone else for everything, and reality itself is increasingly seen in terms of a cosmic conspiracy.

So long as we try to make sense out of life to such a degree in terms of cause and effect, neglecting entirely the larger field of meaning within which particular events occur, the more narrow and vindictive our perception of the world becomes. There is no way we are going to calculate our way out of the costs of high technology. Eventually, we shall have to make a corporate human judgment on

---

4. These comments came five days after the leakage of a chemical poisonous gas from a Union Carbide plant in Bhopal, India, that killed over 2,000 residents. —Ed.

whether we submit the good of the human enterprise to machines or to a loving God. It's not the technology I'm damning here, it's the trust: where we are putting our trust, and what we are doing to ourselves and to others as a result of where we are putting our trust.

From a sermon preached at Christ Church,
Cambridge, MA, December 9, 1984.

META-COMMUNICATION AND CHANGE

The strength of this meta-communication is demonstrated when a professional school attempts to alter its pedagogy to reduce competition. I have experienced the merging of two Episcopal seminaries in which the goal set by a new curriculum emphasized cooperation and community over competition and careerism.[5] Until this time there had been no difference between the pedagogy of the traditional Episcopal seminaries and other graduate schools. With the merger, there was an emphasis on community, and the professors were generally available to students. Indeed, the professors seemed to favor passing students for the sake of community. Few seminarians ever seemed to flunk courses. This sent a message. That seemed to say that the study and the reading and the intellectual enterprise were not very important for parish ministry. The courses were mere obstacles to be overcome in order to pass Canonical Exams (an examination of candidates for ministry required by the candidate's diocese), but not totally relevant for making sense of one's life and work. It was the practical hands-on training of the clinical work (undertaken in mental hospitals, general hospitals, and prisons and developed and supervised by highly skilled institutional chaplains) and not theology, history, biblical study, or ethics that made sense in studying for the ministry.

5. Snow is referring to the 1974 merger of the Philadelphia Divinity School and the Episcopal Theological School in Cambridge, MA to become the Episcopal Divinity School. —Ed.

Nevertheless, by the end of the final semester, the relation-ship between the GOEs,[6] seminary performance, "old boy" con-nections, and bishops came into play. The real "comers" in the class were identified and chosen as assistants by the clergy of large par-ishes. This echelon was followed by the ranks of clergy of upper-middle-class parishes that were wealthy enough to have a curate. Finally, the lower third of the graduates would find their way to rural or urban missions; they learned ministry on their own. In a curious way, Episcopal clergy ended up as ministers to people like themselves, and things went along decently and in order.

But with the suburban boom, the old class system vanished for good. And with this change, the "system" found itself tossed on its ear. What had been small-town, lower-middle-class parishes became rich suburban parishes; the same thing happened to once "lovely country villages." Third-level ministers found their man-ageable ministry overturned by ex-urban growth. "New People" poured into tract housing and brought their children. Additional services were added, as were new wings for Christian education. The expansion vanished almost as suddenly as it had arrived. I sus-pect that this happened because people coming to church really had had hopes of seeing reality defined in terms other than the harshly competitive ones which were causing their growing anxi-ety and sense of isolation. God knows the clergy tried, but their theological education was little help to them in dealing with the true spiritual needs of their growing congregations. When it came to fundraising, the ministers didn't have a clue, and the Social Dar-winist dynamics of professional fundraising took over. Suddenly the air was heavy with such concepts as *strategy*, *big givers*, *success*, and *selling*.

Many clergy—competent, serious ministers of the Gospel—withdrew from such parishes. They didn't like the changes they saw but seemed powerless to stop. In their place came ministers play-ing to win as they had been taught by the meta-communication

6. The General Ordination Examinations were created in 1972 to be an additional written examination to create an academic equivalent to the Law's Bar Exam. —Ed.

of their seminary. Funds were raised and buildings, large and grandiose, were built. In many cases, the funds raised proved to be insufficient; yet the image screamed success. It turned out that the church was a place for winners. Then attendance began to fall off as Gospel authenticity began to disappear. The preaching was usually either purely concerned with social action or unutterably dull stuff laboriously culled out of old seminary notes about a theology the minister had never fully assimilated.

Our seminary had tried to reassess. It was not that the old pedagogy was bad, but that it grew to be in conflict with the Gospel in an increasingly competitive world that its meta-communication seemed to bless. While no one and no group within the church dared to challenge the curriculum openly or to refute its epistemological assumptions, with the withdrawal of support by dioceses, churches, and individuals the message came to us loud and clear: Go back to natural selection and the survival of the fittest.

Thus ministers and doctors and lawyers and scientists and teachers are trained not so much by the content of their discipline as by the structures of their institutions. All relationships are seen as competitive; only competition for survival is sufficient motivation to produce "excellence," "winners," "success," etc. in a world in which we must live. This may be true, but I suspect that if it is, Christianity has been turned on its ear. Certainly the institutions within which we live and work tells us that the truth lies within the survival of the fittest. The extent to which a Christian, or any moral person, can truly identify with and be loyal to such institutions is a frightening question. And yet these institutions are the very climate of our lives.

There was an Irish nun, St. Brigid, who had a vision of heaven as a great hall where the saved sat around a table with Jesus and the twelve, drinking beer throughout eternity. Sounds good to me. Whatever else heaven might be, it is community. It is persons in relationship with God and each other, across the generations and beyond time. It is a communion. Heaven is the ultimate last blessing, the quality of which Matthew describes as the healing of the world and the end of suffering. Those who on earth have suffered from poverty and grief and persecution, will suffer no more as they enter into communion with those on earth who have tried to be just, were compassionate towards the suffering of others, were pure in heart, and worked for peace.

We pray in the Lord's Prayer for a kingdom "on earth as it is in heaven." It is heaven realized. This is our guide as we try to shape a corporate life together here and now. The vision of a divine / human community, spelled out in the gospels helps us to overcome our doubt and despair, and to address the suffering of this world and not to avoid it.

From a sermon preached at Christ Church,
Cambridge, MA, November 6, 1988.

6

The Social Limits of a Sustainable Society

When we speak of a finite planet and the purely physical limits of our global resources, we seem to be dealing with a giant fact which there is no getting around and to which we must respond one way or another. When we speak of social limits, we are not on such hard ground. It is difficult to say with assurance that there are a finite number of behaviors and social interrelationships of which human beings are capable. At times the possibilities seem infinite, that people can do with each other and their environment just about anything they damn well please. In the popular wisdom of Americans, theirs is the greatest country in the world because in America they can do anything they please as long as they don't harm anyone else. "Harm" seems to be interpreted as direct physical damage to other humans or their property, or intentional psychic damage. The assumption is that human beings are, or can and should become, largely independent of one another. To the extent that Americans speak of the common good, they are usually thinking of it in the negative sense of a common "not bad," just as when they think of the law, they think of a sad but necessary compromise with individual human liberty.

All human beings are economically dependent on each other because this dependency is at the heart of our life together on this planet. Since the fifties, we in America have been rebelling against this economic fact of life. We have tried to ensure happiness and success by the extent to which we have achieved economic independence from anyone. With our own house and our own family and our own car and our own savings and investments, we manage our own lives. This way we base most of our human associations on whether we like or dislike someone.

Our wealth, on which we base our independence and privacy, is dependent on massive systems, which themselves in the end, depend on other human beings, many of them poor, angry and outraged by our affluent individualism and privacy. Such is the case with our relationship with the Middle East.

The terror of ambiguity in these tentative times drives us to see things in black and white. We would like life to be right, fair, just, good, and rational. We would like permission to hate all of the opposites of our splendid values, and perhaps permission to destroy them. Our enemies, in their current supreme righteousness, are hateful to us only because they remind us so much of this quality in ourselves. We sustain our righteousness by letting our darker side take over. Slowly and legally and reluctantly we shoot and gas these others and, at home, elect robots.

We speak too much about Christian love as if it existed in an economic vacuum. Christian love is not a luxury; it is the overwhelming realization that our existence, our safety, our very salvation, is tied to the existence, safety, and salvation of our sisters and brothers in the human family. Our job, our vocation, what we are placed here by God to do as Jesus came here to do, is not to root out and destroy that evil and darkness and cruelty in the world or in our own hearts, it is to let it be redeemed by love. The terrible rupture between them and us will never be healed by force, although force will be used again and again. Our vocation

as Christians is to wait and to care, to suffer and to rec-
oncile, to risk and to take the cost in the assurance of the
power of the God of love. God knows that this might be a
fleeting glimpse of God's reality.

As troop carriers and helicopters land in one of the
diminishing number of countries where they may be welcome, we must remember that you and I and the rest of
the world are in the same boat and that we can no longer
base most of our human associations on whether we like or
dislike someone who is different from us.

From a sermon preached at Christ Church,
Cambridge, MA, November 11, 1979.

Americans, then, look upon the corporate nature of the human
enterprise with considerable mistrust as something that makes
only minimal and necessary demands upon the individual, and
even these demands the individual should feel free to question.
The law, too, is not regarded as a good but as a compromise with
the good and something that people obey or disobey according to
how they interpret a given situation. These attitudes no doubt have
their philosophical origins in Locke and Rousseau and the Bill of
Rights, but the near absence of historical imagination in Americans makes the philosophical basis for these attitudes irrelevant.
Americans have undisciplined and unreflective attitudes, more felt
than understood, and not carefully thought out ideas.

Historians and sociologists are quick to point out that these
attitudes are part of our frontier inheritance. When interpersonal
relationships became too complex and demanding, one could always move a little further West, or when one's enterprise began to
conflict with the stricter enforcement of the law, one could move
to a less organized territory. The multinational corporation and
the Swiss bank account are a part of this same frontier tradition.
One comes to see the corporate good and the law as adversaries to
be outsmarted when they conflict with one's growth and success,
but not as enemies, since one will inevitably need their protection. This curious ambivalence was evidenced in the Watergate

matter, where those involved honestly thought of themselves as "good Americans" and were regarded as such by their powerful constituency. These men were eager to encourage legislation that protected their own interests and those of their constituencies (oil, agribusiness, and the military-industrial complex), and were even willing to use agencies of law enforcement for their own political aggrandizement and to talk passionately of law and order, while in those areas where their interests and the law conflicted, they either circumvented the law or broke it.

The great banana hoax has not been properly understood. It was a carefully planned, beautifully executed practical joke that was placed on the whole country and was treated seriously by *Time* and *Life* magazines. In strategic places those counter-culture characters we call "hippies" began buying bananas, scraping and drying the insides of the skins and smoking them. There are absolutely no hallucinogenic ingredients in banana skins, but experts who were called in found chemicals similar in the basic structure to hallucinogens; they could not say that there was no hallucinogenic effect. Suddenly the banana, the most harmless and popular of fruits, became the enemy. Government officials began seriously and publically to conjecture on how they could be banned.

Now hippiedom was splitting its collective sides over the success of this little joke, but as one pointed out to me, the success of the joke was a little scary. He said, "I didn't think myself that so many people were this uptight, and scared and paranoid. When you think these people have the hydrogen bomb, it scares you."

They have a point. This kind of primitive over-reaction is becoming to be the hallmark of American life. It is making the entire world nervous to see this kind of infantile reaction to nearly every domestic problem in our country. They see us beefing up our police forces and National Guard to deal with the turbulence in our cities, rather than trying to deal rationally with the causes of this turbulence.

They see us wondering how to ban the banana. But they don't laugh; they shiver. For they know, too, that our present foreign policy is to police the entire world with the same magnifying glass. It might be wise to reexamine our international commitments as it becomes clear that we cannot deal rationally with many of the most pressing domestic problems. Whatever else hippies do, they do us a great favor by continuously exposing us to ourselves and to the world how jittery we are, and how deeply we need to reexamine our values and priorities as a nation.

From a sermon preached at Christ Church,
Cambridge, MA, October 15, 1967.

Yet today [the seventies], if one can believe the polls, there are still millions of Americans who cannot, for the life of them, figure out what all the fuss was about. These people argue that all the same things were done by politicians and presidents of the past and their respective crews, only more discreetly and on a smaller scale. The style was American, in the truest sense of the word, except that they got caught, and this suggests that they were not as smart as they should have been. That they got caught is a very important consideration. The law is so seldom regarded, in America, any longer as a paradigm for just, reasonable, and consensually validated limits on human behavior. It is, instead, perceived by many as an elegant and mysterious defense the privileged have rigged for themselves against a majority of their fellow citizens. Yet a society without limits is a contradiction in terms.

There must be limits of some kind in a society as viable as ours, for no society exists without some sort of theoretical or pragmatic model that demands limits. For Americans, the limits are regarded as inherent in progress through natural selection. Our model is basically Darwinist and evolutionary, and the limits are seen as those natural restrictions forced upon behavior by competition for survival. The limits of American society are the limits put upon the behavior of a running back by a defensive end. They are part of the process we have pretty much agreed to live by, whereby the basic relationship is the adversarial relationship, and all other relationships are subordinate to that.

The goal of life is survival or one of survival's metaphors: success, victory, winning. The proper limits for human behavior emerge from the fear of failure: losing, defeat, or death. What one does not do is that which is likely to fail; what one does is that which is most likely to success. Within this system, freedom is the freedom to choose the area within which one will succeed or fail. Within this area, "winning is not the most important thing, winning is the only thing."[1] Competence, performance, and technique (all metaphors for survival skills) become matters of obsessional concern. To be human within the Darwinist model is to be competent, which is, in turn, to be competitive, which is, in turn, to be a success or a winner, which is, finally, to survive. Within the arena of competition, behavior tends to be over-reactive, grandiose, and out of scale. Where fear of death in whatever metaphorical disguise becomes the primary motivation for human behavior, the concept of growth takes on exaggerated significance, as does the need for control, measurement, and quantification. Growth is regarded as the essential ingredient of a successful enterprise, whether it is the personal growth of an individual, or the economic or numerical growth of a business, university, church, or a medical practice. Anything not growing tends to be regarded as dying, and dying is to be avoided at all costs. In social evolution, dying is for losers.

A caveat for understanding "growth" comes from the field of medicine. People don't like to hear from their doctors that they have a "growth," and very quickly they want to know if it is benign or malignant. Cancer represents insane, unlimited growth. It has metaphorical significance in the fields of politics and technology, where a fear of mindless and limitless growth creates an obsession with calculation and control. Yet calculation, with its assumption of accurate prediction, gives the illusion of control simply in the doing.[2] The substitution of calculation for judgment does not of-

1. This quote is one of two variations attributed to UCLA Bruins Football coach Henry Russell "Red" Saunders in 1950. —Ed.

2. Colonialism has always worn the badge of expansion. —Ed.

ten lead to real boundaries on human action, but rather to those pragmatic limits which promise successful growth for some enterprise that is currently working well. Alas! The promise is seldom kept.

VIETNAM

As painful as the subject is, the Vietnam War must be considered if one is to reflect seriously on the failure of limits and the absence of a sense of finitude in American society. The geopolitical assumption behind our decision to take over from the French was that communism was a kind of undifferentiated ideological cancer. It is important to note that this deeply felt, partly irrational assumption was the basis for American intervention in Vietnam. Almost immediately after the election of President Kennedy, foreign policy experts began to question this assumption on the basis of deteriorating relationships between China and Russia and a close observation of how, in the communist world, ideology became so quickly subordinated to nationalism. The assumption on which the decision to intervene had been made was, then, if not disapproved, at least seriously questioned. On the basis of the original assumption, the intervention made at least as much sense as the intervention in Korea; the original intervention in Vietnam was limited and tentative, and with good reason, since it had no UN sanction whatsoever and was essentially unilateral.

I am utterly obsessed with the utter failure of communication between those for and those against Vietnam. I am convinced that this failure of communication is a symptom of a far deeper failure of communication that has existed for at least several centuries, which affects every aspect of Western Society, and which is, at its core, a theological conflict.

It fascinates me that conservatives are split over Vietnam, Socialists are split over Vietnam, families are split over Vietnam, political parties are split over Vietnam, preachers are split over Vietnam, denominations are split over Vietnam, religions are split over Vietnam. Clearly, where one stands on the Vietnam War is an article of faith, an article of belief. It has to do with what one believes about humankind. Since the High Middle Ages, this conflict has not been resolved by calling Pelagius a heretic, or stopping the sale of indulgences, or firing Abelard, or exiling Ann Hutchinson, or shooting John Kennedy. The theological conflict is about humankind and our expectations of God. Are we free and responsible? How free? Is God dead? Do we need internal controls grounded by guilt and fear?

The classic faith assumption of Western Christendom is that we are unredeemed and totally depraved. It is a very dark view. Two forms of government speak to this doctrine of man quite clearly: absolute monarchy demanding total obedience, which suggests that order alone, kept by any brutal method, is always more desirable than disorder and, strangely enough, this same system turned topsy-turvy political democracy, which assumes that men are far too evil ever to be trusted by absolute authority and that a system of complicated checks and balances be set up to keep any man or group of men from getting too much power. Democracy is built less on trust in the wisdom of people than it is on distrust of the responsibility of an elite to anyone but themselves. Selfish and power-hungry men will, in the context of party politics, cancel out each other's evil. To risk trusting any mass of men to make religious, political, or moral decisions without the most elaborate system of controls is utter madness. The sinfulness of man requires the tightest controls, otherwise man will live in a dog-eat-dog anarchy. This has been the prevailing teaching of the church, Protestant and Catholic, certainly since Anselm and possibly even earlier.

And so both sides of the schism believe, and believe deeply, that theirs is the Christian position, and let's face it, General Westmorland[3] has far more Christian tradition

---

3. William Westmoreland (1914–2005) was in charge of military

on his side than The Rev. William Sloane Coffin.[4] Both men have impeccable credentials. Both have shown their competence, their physical and moral courage, their honor, their dedication to their country and especially to their faith assumptions. Both are thoroughly decent, kind human beings. One is a national hero; the other will most certainly be thrown in jail. One believes that his Christian responsibility demands that he put harsh controls on the aggressive tendencies of his enemies. The other believes that harsh controls will simply make our enemies more impulsively and irrationally our enemies when our enemies could be met pretty much like ourselves, and our common interests could in the long run be made the agenda of our relationship.

One is made a hero; one goes to prison. Both are Christians. This is the dilemma we face. I think it is a matter to study.

From a sermon preached at Christ Church,
Cambridge, MA, January 28, 1968.

Hindsight forces us to ask why the American leadership chose to involve us in a disaster of such epic proportions. The assumption that communism was a monolithic Marxist-Leninist ideological conspiracy to take over the world had no compelling validity. Clearly no decision was made, no human judgment. The chaos that followed was based on a kind of survival terror,

operations in Vietnam from 1964–1968. Believing that the war should be extended into Cambodia and Laos, he was called back to serve as US Army Chief of Staff. He was devoted member of the Episcopal Church.—Ed.

4. The Rev. William Sloane Coffin, Jr. (1924–2006) was a civil rights and peace activist. He was chaplain at Yale University and became Senior Minister at the Riverside Church in New York City. Coffin stood solidly against the war in Vietnam and upon the death of Martin Luther King was called the "inheritor of King's mantle." While arrested and jailed three times between 1961 and 1964 for civil rights protests in Alabama, Georgia, and Florida, Coffin never spent long in incarceration. In 1968, Coffin was found guilty of conspiring to aid and abet draft resistance, which brought with it an extended sentence; the charge was appealed and overturned.—Ed.

the impulsivity of which was disguised as rational calculation. As President Lyndon Johnson explained to the troops in Korea on his way to Vietnam, "The trouble is that there are only two hundred million of us and nearly three billion of them and you and I know why we're here. They want what we got, and we're not going to give it to them."[5] It was this same president, whose pockets were crammed with computer read-outs projecting an optimistic end to the conflict, who promised at press conferences that there was light at the end of the tunnel.

The most distinctive thing about Vietnam was its excess, the absence of any scale or proportion. The kind of hysterical techno-logical overkill employed to fight this war was without precedent. The saturation bombing, the massive use of helicopters, the mind-less yet very intentional use of defoliants, and the utter absence of any coherent thought for the consequence of "winning," the only expressed goal of the war, all of these things, in retrospect, would seem to be pure insanity. When one adds to this the assurances of the government that such a war could be fought without disrupt-ing the American economy, one shudders with disbelief.

Neither is it reassuring that concurrently with the war, pro-fessional football overtook baseball as the national sport and be-gan to rely increasingly on medical technology (amphetamines, steroids, and special orthopedic surgery) and million dollar con-tracts to create the basic American paradigm for human existence. Without football metaphors, our politicians would be speechless. Nor is it altogether a coincidence that after the oil crisis of 1972 and the slump in automobile sales and the economy generally, the major car companies clawed their way back to the greatest profits in history by producing small economical cars which, in just a few years, would be easily and expensively accessorized with just about anything. Excess is alive and well in America.

It is my contention, then, that behind much of the over-reactive, excessive behavior of America lies a kind of nuclear-age survival terror which is repressed or denied or rationalized, and

5. Taken from President Johnson's address to the troops at Camp Stanley, Korea, on November 1, 1966.—Ed.

which then proceeds to pervade every aspect of our common life, and our lives as individuals as well. It goes far beyond what in the past has been regarded as a normal fear of death. It has more to do with the death of the future, the death of hope.

Metanoia is the Greek word that refers to a change in mind, a different way of thinking. Metanoia is the opposite of paranoia. We cannot seem to learn the basic lesson of the New Testament and of history that fear is the cause of paranoid behavior. At its heart, it is the assumption that each person is a potential adversary of every other person. The more frightened I am, the more angry and defensive I get, the more I imagine the person causing my anger and defensiveness is angry with me. The more I imagine this anger in another, the more my behavior becomes defensive and hostile toward others, and the more that that happens, the more frightened and angry others become toward me. Paranoid feelings are apt to cause runaway escalation.

Fear. We can brood about mutual assured destruction and nuclear holocaust and the destruction of the planet literally until doomsday, but such brooding will not lead us toward nuclear disarmament. It may well do the opposite. I am no longer deluded into security by the thought that every problem has a solution. But I do wonder how Christians are to exist with this problem as we attempt to diminish its likelihood. The nuclear fat is in the fire. The bombs and their delivery systems exist, and they exist within a complex system that includes all of us and affects every aspect of our lives. Only love can cast out fear and allow us the luxury of metanoia. As the great German theologian Dorothee Soelle once wrote, "In Jesus Christ, God disarmed himself. God surrendered himself without arms to those who keep crying for more and more protection and arms. In Jesus Christ, God renounced violence, and of course he did this unilaterally, without waiting for us to lay down our weapons first."[6]

6. Soelle, *Choosing Life*, 87.

I Win, We Lose

From a sermon preached at Christ Church,
Cambridge, MA, July 11, 1982.

In John Updike's short story regarding life in the fifties, "When Everyone was Pregnant," the narrator comments:

> Our fat fifties cars, how we loved them, revved them: no one thought of pollution. Exhaust smoke, cigarette smoke, factory smoke, all romantic. Romance of consumption at its height. Shopping for baby food in the gaudy trash of the supermarkets. Purchasing power: young, newly powerful, born to consume. To procreate greedily. A smug conviction that the world was doomed. Beyond the sparkling horizon, an absolute enemy. Above us, bombs whose flash would fill the scene like a cup to overflowing.[7]

The fear has increased since the fifties; it has become the hidden, pervasive terror that motivates the insane rebellion of Western humanity against its own finitude and the finitude of the planet.

Nuclear war is an oxymoron; it contradicts itself. War is a contest between two nations in which each hopes by force to prove that its interpretation of historical reality is correct. Nuclear missiles are not weapons. Their use has no function in what we understand to be warfare. Yet how we deal with them is dictated by our traditional understanding of warfare. We see the build-up of nuclear weapons and the improvement of their technology as arming ourselves against the enemy, as a traditional arms build-up that, if warfare should break out, would assure our winning, as the guardian of our interpretation of historical reality.

As this kind of thinking goes on and on, and the threat grows rather than diminishes, the mind, in moments of clarity, sees that the whole purpose of building more and more missiles and warheads is not to have to use them. They become symbols of something confused and ambiguous.

7. Updike, *Museums and Women*, 93.

Because we *cannot* bear the reality of what we are doing, we have turned the unreal concept of nuclear war *into a game*, like chess. The bishop is not a bishop, or a king a king: all are, in the end, symbolic pawns of our intellect. But the focus of our intellectual energy is on the survival of our own king and the destruction of our opponent's king. It is important to notice that chess, the most intellectual of all games, may also involve the most passion. Behind all that intellectualizing is a deep primal obsession with combat, patricide, survival, and God only knows what else that lies within our murky psychic depths.

This is all harmless enough done with small pieces of wood or ivory on a board. But when, by game theory, we see it being replicated in the development of strategies for nuclear war, we are beginning to think the unthinkable.

From a lecture given at Christ Church,
Cambridge, MA, November 9, 1986.

The space program has given us a growing awareness that our planet is a complex but finite ecosystem. What we knew intellectually was validated with felt, visual impact. The earth is a small planet, self-contained, maintaining an impossible, living equilibrium in the midst of nothing definably alive at all. The systemic limits within which the human enterprise must take place are defined beyond argument. The kind of technological mobilization needed to colonize space would destroy the planet before it could take place. Time has become our most rapidly diminishing resource. We are mortal not just as individuals, but as a species, and the planet is mortal as well.

The excessive, over-reactive behavior of Americans takes place within the ambience of a felt consciousness of the planet's ecosystem, an ecosystem threatened at all times by war. Within this ambience, the question asked so far is *not* how humans can live together equitably, gratefully, lovingly during the time given to us to be alive; the question asked is "Who is most fit to survive?" Until Darwin, survival was a short-term concept referring to discreet events. Its cosmic application is meaningless, as is the cosmic application of all pragmatic terms.

Such words as winning, success, victory—or their antonyms, losing, failure, defeat—are also pragmatic terms; that is, referring to discrete *pragma*, acts, events which have beginnings and ends within a discrete individual human life, or a discrete human generation, both of which have their own beginnings and ends. We can say that the Israelis won the Six-Day War, that they were successful in that war, that they were victorious in that war. But really they feel like *survivors* in the most accurate sense of the word. Their survival is full of tragic memory, current anxiety, and vivid apprehension; they know the tentativeness of winning, victory, and even of survival itself.

The giving of cosmic significance to pragmatic concepts breaks down any systemic apprehension of reality, and by reducing reality to a random linear accretion of discrete symbolic events all categorized as either winners or losers, successes or failures leading to survival or death, removes all scale and proportion from human existence. Americans confuse the Olympic Games with foreign policy, a presidential election with the World Series or the Super Bowl, Disneyland with history, and television with reality.

Alienated from nature and Eden by our own consciousness and doomed to the unique consciousness of our own deaths, we would love to be one with nature again, but that is not given to us. Set apart from nature by God, we gaze upon nature's ravishing complexity and orderliness and beauty, knowing all the time that nature does not care at all about what happens to us, but is simply and mindlessly calling us back to the dust. If we cannot be painlessly a part of nature, perhaps, we reason, we can manage nature, dominate it, overcome, and subjugate it. Well, perhaps we can, but probably not without killing it and ourselves as well. Having used so much of it up to dominate it, we have decided to change it by splicing a few genes. If we cannot

feel safely a part of nature, we can at least manage nature
and arrange it according to our whims.

From a sermon preached at Christ Church,
Cambridge, MA, May 5, 1982.

AMERICAN VALUES

One wonders what happens as a result of this confusion. One critically important result is a takeover of the American value system
by the media, particularly by television. At the risk of belabor-
ing the obvious, it must still be said that the primary purpose of
American TV, to which every other purpose is subordinate, is the
selling, not so much of specific products as a value system based
on survival through consumption. This is accomplished by defining the lifestyle of a winner. What a winner buys is a winning product, a product that beats all other "leading competitors" in various
forms of excellence: performance, beauty, style, texture, flavor, etc.
The TV audience is treated to the edifying spectacle of absorbency
contests between rival paper towels. American automobile manu-
facturers take on European brands while more than a few European brands disdain competition with anyone. In America, most
European cars are for the leader or the intellectual winner, not for
crass commercial types. Through all this, consumption is defined
as a form of intelligent aggression. In the act of buying, one not
only confirms that one is a winner by identifying with a winning
product, but also, by a single decisive stroke, relegates all competing products to the agony of defeat. The shopping experience is
designed to have one emerge a winner with the assurance of his or
her consumer competence.

The same Darwinist value system pervades the entire range
of television programming. Presidential campaigns, the Olympics,
situation comedies, and cop shows are portrayed as what "America
is all about," and what America is all about is winning. Commenta-
tors inform their audience that the presidential party platform's

content is and always has been irrelevant since the framing of that platform is subordinated to strategies of winning. Interviews with Olympians are made with those whom the network has calculated will win the gold medal. Later, we may see one of them accepting the bronze with tears of failure streaming down his or her face. "Sitcoms" portray an extended family of born losers who teach us the fine art of the put-down as they build an arena where they can win their micro-victories. Cop shows reveal that the law is a hindrance to law enforcement officers in their blood feud with criminals. Their dirty job of being shot, beaten up, overworked, deserted by their wives, and betrayed by their comrades is the story, not of their winning but rather of survival. Cop shows themselves survive the ratings better than less violent offerings. Is this what "America it is all about?"

At issue here with television are the possible consequences of their programs and their advertising. One would first expect a widespread depression of the viewing public. Since winning, or success, or survival are not true existential categories (there are no winners or successes or survivors), then one must expect that people who measure the value of their lives against these life goals will come to believe that something is seriously wrong with them, that they are failures and utterly worthless. Since depression is hostility turned inward, the alienating behavior of a person who sees all relationships in competitive terms would result in self-loathing.

A second result, if the depression indeed exists, would be impulsive, manic behavior involving excessive and indiscriminate consumption, grandiose projects, and excessive energy expended in a kind of erratic busyness. This kind of compensatory behavior, although it is often mixed with long periods of apathy and passivity, is, of course, what advertisers are trying hard to trigger. There is considerable evidence that depressed people tend to buy more of everything than those people who are feeling reasonably cheerful. There seems to be evidence of a growing depression in the population. Newspaper headlines periodically remind us that alcoholism in America is reaching epidemic proportions. One notices among men and women in their fifties a sudden and alarming rise in the consumption of alcohol. Epidemic alcoholism then, to the extent that it has depression as a major part of its etiology, suggests that depression is itself reaching epidemic proportions. As for impulsive, indiscriminate consumption, one only has to examine a common enough reaction to the economic recession brought on by the 1973–1974 Arab oil embargo. The economy's two worst years since the Great Depression were the two most prosperous years in the history of Florida's tourism.

Further, impulsivity is not related solely to consumption. Some of our very large and reputable banks, famous in the past for their conservative investment policies, have been engaged in a surprising number of high-risk investments, many of which have not panned out. The obsession with rapid growth as the prime indicator of economic health, has as a result, caused a failure of judgment affecting economic panic when the economy falters or slows down.

A third result one might expect would be a radical diminishment of institutional loyalty, a loyalty which demands that limits be put upon the needs and desires of the individual for the corporate good. Courses and workshops on assertiveness training and publications like "Moneysworth" signal the theme of averting institutional victimization. Institutional loyalty equals the reduction of personal options, whereas the employee believes that one should keep as many options as possible open. As the beer advertisement suggests, "You only go around once in life so you've got to grab for all the gusto you can."[8]

Television and the media, therefore, are responsible for selling an intrinsically self-destructive value system that has set person against person in competition for success, as well as to define this "success," entirely in terms of massive consumption. If limits are a reflection on how humans apprehend reality, the destruction of these limits in the definition of success and survival distorts this apprehension of reality so as to make humanity its own worst enemy. One might say its influence is demonic.

8. This was the slogan of the Schlitz Brewing Company's 1971 advertisement campaign. —Ed.

The Judeo-Christian tradition holds that the impulse to accumulate or squander material goods, rather than the impulse to use and enjoy them, is a violation of stewardship of what has been given to us. In opposition to this, the media seeks to teach us that the accumulation of and impulsive waste of material goods is the ultimate measurement of human value. This conflict stands between humankind and its health and wholeness.

The Judeo-Christian tradition holds that The Law is a gift of a loving and trustworthy God. Conversely, the media teaches that the law justifies the powerful in their fitness to survive and creates a model for us to follow as the right use of Social Darwinism.

Where the Judeo-Christian tradition has seen existence as the natural cycle of birth, growth, maturity, diminishment, and death enabling the birth of new life, the media present a preposterous growth–death dichotomy that devastates the scale and proportion of human existence.

Where the Judeo-Christian has maintained that intelligent aggression should be tempered and modified to serve the common good, the media teaches that intelligent aggression is the primary shaping force of the cosmos.

That organized religion in America has failed in every way to identify and confront the unreality of the media's message can only suggest that at a profound, felt level a majority of Christians and Jews have come to accept it and to make their daily decisions on the assumption that it is true. Never before in history has such a chasm existed between professed belief and practicing belief, and it is out of this chasm that our religious anomie or hysterical evangelism flows.

The precise situation that creates fascism is where society is demoralized, where the conscientious are paralyzed with guilt and leadership believes that it is no longer accountable to anyone, where social disorder is everywhere and that this disorder is everywhere met with more police using more force. It occurs when the law is set aside in the name of order and humans find that the fear, the tension, the chaos, and the guilt become unbearable. It is at that moment when the human spirit is tempted to say suddenly, "No! Wrong is right, evil is good, ugliness is beauty, repression is true freedom, and the important thing is to be on the side of the strong. This is nature's law—the weak, the stupid, the ugly, all those people who are not like me are destined to be destroyed, they are a drag on us, the truly strong. We've wasted enough time on them—let's get it over with—why put up with their nonsense?" And so we have Kent State, Attica, Baton Rouge, Hanoi, Haiphong, Laos, and Cambodia. They say, "Next, it may be the major cities in our own country." Newark today is in worse shape than Hanoi and far more demoralized. The same people are responsible for the devastation in both cities.

There seems to be a new role for Christians in America, an ironic one. It seems to be our vocation to be strangers in our own land, aliens in our own land, in what we regard as our own home. Christians don't see what others see: what gives them hope gives us pain, what others want, we detest, what others call "loyalty," we call "apostasy." Increasingly, the majority is beginning to refer to us as "imbecilic." But we are by nature Apocalyptic. What seems to be chaos is truly judgment; all order from force is chaos and destruction. We await a New Jerusalem.

From a sermon preached at Christ Church,
Cambridge, MA, January 7, 1973.

For Christians, then, the first step in a revision of Christian tradition is self-examination to discover the extent to which we have come to confuse salvation with survival and holiness with fitness to survive. To do this is to throw oneself into a painful tension with American society that in our time is an absolute condition of valid prayer. It is only in the pain of this tension, blessed and focused and made significant by prayer, that a revision of tradition will find sacramental expression in new patterns of corporate life. The Christian community must become, like the early church, an alternative community where survival is recognized as entirely within the purview of a loving God, and the business of Christians becomes mutual care and concern in an atmosphere of prayerful attention as they serve each other and the world. As they wait, they will develop a politics of witness based on a vision of reality which will, in time and eternity, assert its claim upon the whole of creation. For the creation is whole, indeed holy, and human holiness is in a cooperative relationship to it all.

A few weeks ago I drove down to Cambridge to hear Bishop Tutu, Archbishop Emeritus of South Africa, speak. I have seldom in my life been so moved, in part because he gave me a way to look at Justification that was balanced and compassionate. He had been appointed chair of a commission to whom white people, who had been working on behalf of the apartheid government, were publically permitted to confess to the dreadful things they had done. They had murdered and tortured blacks for no apparent reason except to keep the government intact. Their choice was between this public confession or standing trial in the traditional way. If they chose to confess publically, they were set free.

What they confessed to was too horrible to mention, but what most appalled Bishop Tutu was the way a person whose official job was torture and execution could be a good family man, happily married with a number of children, who regularly went to church on Sunday. Such a man could confess in a flat, unemotional voice that he was just doing his job. Other men, confessing similar crimes would do so sobbing uncontrollably. The families of those tortured and killed were permitted to attend the confessions and likewise were wracked with sobs, but many were willing to speak to the executioners after their confessions and forgive them.

For these African Christians, forgiveness was more than just a theological doctrine. A whole judicial system was set up based upon it. Those who, by faith, repented, faced who they were and what they'd done were forgiven. No attempt was made to distinguish between those whose confessions were the result of deep remorse and those who made a slick effort to get off "scot-free." Those who believed that their lives were justified by doing their duty were not punished. They were simply allowed to live with themselves in their self-constructed hell.

The procedure was not neat and clean like a legal trial or like simple revenge. The procedure was fitted to the human heart, with all the flexibility and ambiguity of the human heart. But when we compare it to revenge, the real best and clean problem solver, it makes reconciliation possible; it can bring the merry-go-round of hating and killing to an end. It proves that the endless slaughter we find around the world is not inevitable, if we have the courage to be really reconciled to God and our neighbor.

From a sermon preached at St. John's Church,
Ashfield, MA, undated (1999–2000).

7

Death and the Possible Rebirth of Love

In contemporary Western industrial society, one word has more power than any other. It is used in all dire prophecy; it is used to justify every action. It is used to motivate and control and hold together the entire corporate enterprise of the West. The word is *survival*, an inter-psychic response to terror in the face of death.

It is impossible to say when survival terror began its invasion of Western Christendom. Galileo's discovery that our planet was not at the center of the universe did not discourage many from living in the three-storied universe that had Biblical warrant. Newton's discovery that all matter was cooling off, wearing out, slowing down, dying, was relegated to the safe, theoretical world of science and ignored by all but a few intellectuals. The Rev. Thomas Malthus's warning that humans would overpopulate themselves out of cosmic house and home caused some minor stir at the time, and may have penetrated Western consciousness more than has been generally understood. It most certainly penetrated the consciousness of Charles Darwin and was, perhaps, the critical factor in Darwin's conclusion that natural selection was the central dynamic of evolution. The species with the most adaptive behavior survive. The rest, nature kills off. It is unfortunate that this theory surfaced in the midst of an industrial economy that found its rationale in Adam Smith.

It was not Darwin but Herbert Spencer who coined the phrase "the survival of the fittest," and probably no social theory in history ever found currency so quickly. In England and America, Spencer's "Social Darwinism" became the basic rationale for laissez-faire capitalism and all forms of imperialism from Rule Britannia to Manifest Destiny. In the United States it pervaded every level of intellectual life: the universities, the public schools, and even churches, once they stopped their doomed argument with Darwin over creation. What is most important to note about Social Darwinism is that, out of the thousands of modes of adaptive behavior, only intelligent aggression was seized upon as appropriate for humans. It is also important to note that Darwin never said that competition for survival within a single species was adaptive behavior; the "survival of the fightingest" is a piece of sociological revisionism.

It should finally be noted that Social Darwinism was not a gloomy or fear-haunted social philosophy to those who held it, namely, those who considered themselves the fittest. Particularly in a large, under-populated country with apparently endless natural resources like the United States, Social Darwinism blended with the concept of progress and was often applied to American democracy as a whole as most fit and destined to survive in the competition of social systems and nations. Both in the United States and in England after World War I, Social Darwinism faded fast in all but the most reactionary. Obviously the fittest, fittest precisely in Social Darwinist terms, had not survived World War I.

In Germany, however, a nation that conceived of itself as crowded, humiliated, cut off from natural resources, and which was indeed suffering from inflation, unemployment, and general social chaos, survival seemed a real issue. But as Konrad Lorenz said ruefully of his cooperation with the Nazi Party, "None of us as much as suspected that the word 'selection,' when used by these rulers, meant 'murder.'"[1] For the first time, Social Darwinism was seized upon with a passionate seriousness and given scientific sanction with the dreadful results that are now history. A group who deemed themselves a superior race put their technological genius coldly to use slaughtering a group they regarded as an inferior race, while another nation using the same technological and scientific genius, a genius born and cultivated in Germany, proceeded to develop a bomb which intensified in every possible way the survival terror of the world. The atomic age had begun and was justified entirely on the level of survival. Geo-politics were frankly and brutally defined in a single phrase, the "balance of terror."

In our own country and in the world, more and more people are being made marginal, pushed to the edge by a prosperous, thriving elite. But turning this issue on its head, who is more marginal at this moment than our leaders? We are locked in the Persian Gulf where all of our decisions are the wrong decisions. We are locked into an economic policy that the whole world is coming to see as destructive to the world economic order. Attacked by the press that presses the politicians into positions that they would gladly abandon as their authority and credibility diminishes.

We can see our appearance as a kind of a cosmic fluke, a random biological event of no importance to anyone else but ourselves. If we do, we can try to claw our way to a position of power and prosperity and security at the center of the mainstream and we possibly succeed. We may call this "survival" and "success," but eventually we shall die. Life seen as one long struggle to avoid the margin, is really one long struggle toward the margin, lived in reaction to the margin, in fear of the margin.

Or, in Jesus, we can see an alternative to this and follow a different path to find the faith and hope to accept our marginality. Believing that we are not here by mistake or chance but by the will of God who loves us, we can dare to

---

1. Lorenz, "1973 Nobel Prize Biographical Statement," paragraph 10.

see ourselves in the faces of the marginal and we can live to maintain a world of trust and mutual concern where marginality itself becomes a basis for community and hope.

If the American mainstream can be persuaded to see its own face in the face of the marginal, to feel its own pain is the pain of the marginal, to understand that its fear is in no sense different from that fear experienced by the marginal, then perhaps all of us will come to see that in our shared marginality we are blessed forever.

From a sermon preached at Christ Church,
Cambridge, MA, October 18, 1987.

It was not long before the West suffered another blow to its inner cosmology. Sputnik was launched and the vastness and coldness of Galileo's universe left the theoretical realm of science and suddenly became a felt reality for all humans. A new panic spread through the West, particularly through the United States. Soon, we were told, gangs of satellites armed with guided atomic missiles would be passing over New York City every hour. We poured money into our public school system to select out the superior students and guide them through the hard sciences, leaving the education of less gifted students a shambles of neglect. By a tremendous expenditure of money, intelligence, and creative energy we surpassed the Russians in space until we landed on the moon. And there, a very human being took a picture of the planet earth, and we realized that it was a small planet, miraculously covered with life, in the midst of nothing identifiably alive at all. We began to feel the limits of human life, began to count our resources with a new realism and discover that they, too, were finite and, even worse, rapidly diminishing. At last, it became apparent that the survival of humans on planet earth was an open question.

The felt apprehension of our cosmic mortality was a very new thing. It had completely disrupted not only the way we see our values, but also the way we see ourselves in relationship to other humans and to our cosmic environment. There have been many and varied reactions to this shattering event, but at present only one is moving towards a deeply felt consensus in the industrial West. It is not a consensus about what we must do to return the earth safely to the human race. The question, which is most urgent, is "Who is to survive?" The answer that the question dictates is, "Those most fit to survive: Ourselves."

Foreign policy became an extension of the most powerful sector of the private enterprise system, the survival of the system being regarded as identical with the nation as a whole. A disastrous war was fought in Vietnam to prove to the world that we are "winners," survivors in a radically competitive world.[2] None of this happened as a part of a conscious ideological conspiracy. All of it was the impulsive, reactive behavior of a terrified people whose value system had disintegrated and who lacked all the sense of what it means to be human on a planet only recently perceived to be as mortal as humans themselves.

And while the new Social Darwinism has not yet become an explicit political philosophy, it is finding its most articulate converts among university professors, particularly in the fields of socio-biology, ethology, genetics, economics, and philosophy. Social Darwinism was also most powerfully communicated in the pragmatics of our institutional life. From Sputnik on, the Selective Service suddenly became more selective in the Darwinist sense than ever before, drafting the unemployed underclass and selecting the "most fit" for survival not only in terms of surviving the war in Vietnam, but also the economic shambles that followed it. The "most fit" were best prepared for college and exemption from the draft; the "most fit" were predominately white and middle class. Rigid SATs (Scholastic Aptitude Tests) made the selection even more precise.

Perhaps most telling of all was the emergence of professional sports as the central metaphor for reality in American life in the fifties. Winning and losing, success and failure, victory and defeat

2. War is based on the assumption that if we can control others through the fear of death, we can somehow put ourselves in the place of God, say whether one may live or die, taste, at least in the moment of triumph, what it is like to be immortal. Snow, *A Vocation to Risk*, 15–16.

became the only trusted categories of existence, and the primary motivation for work was not to help with the maintenance of a humane society but to succeed, to be a winner.

Winning is meaningless without losing. Success is meaningless without failure. These are highly selective categories as evidenced by those with "born to lose" tattooed on their biceps testify. They have become categories of self-definition as well as ways for defining the other. Winners are defined by the symbolic power of what they own as well as what and how much they consume. The winner lifestyle is the basic image of American advertising.

The consequences of a pervasive Social Darwinist perspective is the aggressive accumulation of natural resources, wealth, and technical-scientific information for the single purpose of denying them to the rest of the world as a guarantee of the survival of those currently self-defined as the most fit, namely, the richest and most powerful. And precisely because this Social Darwinism is *not* an articulated political and economic theory, while still being the ordering force of our institutional life, many people who hold radically differing worldviews find themselves making decisions on a purely survival basis. How many parents do not share their children's fears that a 400 on the SATs will define a child as a loser and lock him or her into a loser's role? How many doctoral candidates choose their thesis topic on the basis of real interest rather than on the basis of what will succeed? How many departments in Federal bureaus are as concerned about the work they were set up to do as they are about polishing their image to survive as a department? An increasingly pervasive fear is becoming the primary motive for decision and action, even among people who consciously hold such motivation in contempt.

And yet, those who most obviously hold such motivation in contempt are Christians. No vision of reality could be more in conflict with what Christians believe, and yet Christians, for the most part, are not behaving any differently than others faced with the current crisis in our society. The survival panic, which sweeps the West, sweeps Christians along with everyone else. It is time, first of all, to understand clearly what we as Christians are going along with, to face what our prevailing motivation is. Next we must decide, not just intellectually, but with our whole hearts, whether we should prefer to accept Social Darwinism as simple reality. It was too bad about the Native Americans. There were many beautiful things about *their* way of life, but *they* were clearly not up to adapting to American society and had to go. Yes, Appalachia was very beautiful, but if one is going to become an industrial nation, one needs coal. The automobile may not have been the perfect choice as a normal mode of transportation, but it has served us well, and the decision was made. We not only have the cars and the roads, but we also have millions of Americans who depend on the automobile for employment.

It is true that we have transformed warfare into such a nightmare of carnage and material waste, into such disposal of human and natural resources . . . but do we want nations who have declared themselves our enemies to thrive? And if our technological mode of warfare has caused a temporary disruption in our economy and reduced our resources of fossil fuel more than we might like, to be as independent as we might like, won't our ingenuity and Yankee know-how pull us through? Face it. There isn't enough to go around on this planet unless we choose to throw away the most comfortable, elegant, liberated life-style in the history of the world and become primitives again. What we're talking about, hyperbolically, is the survival of the American way of life, and there's no reason to believe that a *more equal* distribution of global resources is necessarily a *more just* distribution. It was through our own imagination, creativity, efficiency, and hard work that we achieved our success. We have *earned* the pre-eminent position that we hold on this planet, and we shall continue to hold it as something we justly deserve. Our allies are, in most respects, as well off as we are. As for the rest, they made their choice and they can live with it. It is a simple rule of nature that the most fit survives. There must always be losers.

THE CHALLENGE BEFORE US

The Challenge: Any American above the poverty level in the Unites States today must face the fact that this philosophy of life has been the cause of our unparalleled affluence, even though there is growing evidence that it will not continue to serve us so well, even on a material level. Indeed, this philosophy can be challenged on a purely pragmatic level at many, many points. But for those of us who have profited from it as individuals, it has great visceral cogency, whether we are Christians or not. To forswear it individually, to give it up and drop out, would seem to be the ultimate exercise in futility.

Yet to live with it, for Christians, means to live in a continuing state of inner conflict. Perhaps the most important first step in facing this conflict with the intention of resolving it in repentant commitment is to face it in the most naked theological terms. To be a Christian is to believe that death has no ultimate dominion over the human enterprise. Christianity holds that *both* humans and creation itself are "fallen." Humans have had the knowledge that they should die, and that the earth given to them as their home was a creature like themselves and subject to the same mortal limits. Anything created, anything that has a beginning, has an end, with no final, autonomous say over when that end will come or what its nature will be. This is the absolute boundary of human knowledge. We die and the planet Earth has an end. With these two things humans must exist, having no knowledge or control over either one.

Human consciousness of mortality is not the same as the smoothly adaptive survival instincts of animals which blend into one balanced systemic whole. The majestic cyclic movement of organic life from conception to birth, to growth, to procreation, to maturity, to diminishment, to death may be something which in our saner moments we might desire to join, but which we resist. Human life, lived in the consciousness of mortality, is perceived by most of us as painful, discontinuous, and at times random, often subject to pathos and on occasion willed into tragedy. Its total meaning, its overall significance, is not at all obvious. This information is not conveyed to us by our genes, it must be told to us in words, passed on to us in words from generation to generation, always to be decoded in new circumstances, new circumstances for us as individuals and as part of a generation. One has only to read the Psalms to see how profoundly a part of the Biblical view of the human condition this is.

It was St. Paul who, perhaps more precisely than anyone since, understood how the Christ Event spoke to the painful ambiguity of human life lived in full consciousness of mortality, under the realm of sin and death. It was he who perceived that even The Law, lived under and obeyed out of an obsessive desire to be set apart for salvation, from the ruck of other humans, was an instrument of sin and death. For St. Paul, Jesus the Christ became a single Divine statement about the nature of reality. The coming of the Christ was not so much an intervention of God into history, but instead the revelation of a reality until that moment only partially understood. God had been present in history from the beginning, as had the Christ. Love had not been an unknown quantity in the world before the coming of the Christ, but its apprehension and definition had been at first radically limited. The God of Hebrew Scripture had been a loving and faithful and just God, but His love, and faithfulness, and His justice had been perceived by the Hebrews as revealed only to them. It was revealed first to a clan, and then, in his gracious condescension to them, to an entire people. Even later, the prophets include His sovereignty over the entire world extended this understanding of God.

The writers of Christian scripture were even more aware that the Christ event had made all things new by the breathtaking inclusiveness it revealed in its power to break the iron rule of death. The Messiah himself had died, not just for Israel but for all humanity. The ultimate word to be spoken about Jesus was love, a love so transcendent that a brutal, tortured, humiliating death as a common criminal affected it not at all. It was revealed, as Sister

Mary Corita[3] puts it so simply, that "Love is here to stay, and that's enough."

But this love, as it manifests itself in the corporate life of those who, by faith, regard it as an expression of divine will, who live within its graceful limits, is itself something utterly new. It includes the weak, and the poor, and the sick, and the mad, and the hungry, and the unsheltered, and the imprisoned. It includes the self-declared enemy: it includes the rich and powerful. It goes beyond affection, and sexuality, and kinship bonds, and mutuality and has as its motivating center not survival, but gratitude. It is a kind of grateful wonder at the unearned gift of life itself and a need to share oneself and what one is given with one's neighbor out of this gratitude.

Gratitude, it has always seemed to me, is something we are taught to fake. I can remember my mother telling me to say "thank you for the lovely party" to my little host and his mother as I left two hours of the most terrifying chaos I had experienced in all of my five years. If gratitude is a feeling, I doubt that children feel it. If "thank you" is taught as a piece of rhetoric, we are too often as children taught to attach it to the wrong moment.

I think of the old Danny Kaye record where he mimics a little boy saying as he writes Christmas thank-you notes, "Dear Aunt Alice, Thank you very much for the underwear." Children, for the most part, seem to believe that whatever good happens to them is only what they deserve.

I once was a fellow of the Judge Baker pilot project in adjudicated juvenile delinquency.[4] We were assigned two

---

3. Corita Kent (1918–1986) was an artist, educator, and a member of the Order of the Immaculate Heart of Mary. She taught at Immaculate Heart College in Los Angeles, CA, and served as chair of the art department. She was known for her posters, banners, and book covers which reflected themes of love and peace. She designed a US postal stamp and is known for creating the unique decoration that adorns the Dorchester gas tank near Boston, MA.—Ed.

4. The Judge Baker Program, affiliated with Harvard University, began in 1917. It is an ongoing attempt to use multidisciplinary research to further the

or three kids with whom we would work closely in order to get to know them very well. We were taught that the one thing we could do to help the turning around process was to wait for a neutral moment a month or so into the relationship, and for no reason whatsoever, give the kid five dollars, put an arm around his shoulder, and say, "You're a good kid." I did this twice during my fellowship and the results were utterly astonishing.

In both cases, the delinquent boys grabbed ahold of me, and held on with all their might, sobbing uncontrollably. The five-dollar bill, the hug, and the words came as a total surprise. They could not defend themselves against it because they had never experienced anything like it.

What they experienced was gratitude, not just a feeling, although very much a feeling, but a feeling attached to the sudden, cognitive realization that there was in the world some hidden, unexplainable power that confirmed them as having value just as they were, as human beings.

I think most people have had moments like this: moments of transformational gratitude where deep doubts about our significance, our value, are done away with, and with an exquisite yet powerful gratitude, we realize that there is good reason for our being here. We move from self-doubt and a vague mistrust of others to a sudden conviction that we are somehow, ultimately safe, that life in the end is indeed trustworthy, that we can let ourselves be open to love and to be loved, that we are, in fact, loved and have been since the beginning.

> From a sermon preached at Christ Church,
> Cambridge, MA, October 15, 1995.

This love, as St. Paul knew so well, is far beyond the human capacity to give, and the double wonder of it is that, no matter how flawed, distorted, adulterated, and misguided it may be as the result of the incursions of survival panic upon our attempts to

---

well being of children. —Ed.

practice it, it still is acceptable, still precious to God and humanity simply as it is offered. For the Early Church, as for Jesus himself, Christian love was best understood within the context of a kind of family not based on kinship but on what was then called an *oikos*, or household, a group of people taking responsibility for the welfare of one another which had been previously been reserved for members of a blood family. Yet this household extended to the stranger, the traveler, the beggar, the same care which held together its own corporate life. This household was the very real, historical basic human unit of the Early Church, but at the same time it became a model for the Kingdom of God, a model for how God intended humans to live upon Earth until the last day.

Because the last day was expected and hoped for momentarily, the result was an extraordinary willingness to put up with the messiness and the conflicts within, and the dangers of indiscriminate concern for any "neighbor" without who happened along. The consciousness of mortality was transformed by faith in Jesus, from a source of greed, self-deceit, competitive ruthlessness, and blind hatred into the guiding motive of a cheerful companionship of the pilgrims moving toward the consummation of their corporate joy. They knew exactly why they had been born and what they intended to do with the life which had been given to them. The end was in God's hands and God was love.

If we read the Book of the Acts of the Apostles or St. Paul's Letters, we discover that the society that emerged from this vision of reality was far from perfect. It was too open a social system to be peaceful or even orderly. Its equilibrium was constantly disrupted by wandering charismatics with their compelling dreams and visions, by fits of persecution by the Roman government, harsh doctrinal disagreements among church leaders, and all the problems of cultural lag which occur when people of different backgrounds are brought together by a new vision of reality. But certain primary values of the community held firm through it all. It was simply and thoroughly understood that, until the last day, people were not left to starve while others ate from their surplus. The aged, sick, and infirm were not to be left unattended. Children were to be cared for. Force was not to be an ordering principle of corporate life. The basic resources of the earth were to be shared, not accumulated or squandered. Special attention was to be given to the most alienated: to prisoners, to the insane, to lepers and cripples. Christianity was not a religion for winners. It was not concerned with success when it was most truly what it had been created to be. It was in the world to love. Survival was entrusted to God; it was not within the purview of humankind.

Christians, then, as in the past, must not be over-concerned with the survival of the human race. They must believe that they have no more control over it than they do over their own survival as individuals. They believe that their task is to make the human corporate life on this planet as just and loving as they can with God's help for as long as it is given them to do so. Their vision of reality is a cosmic household, a lively, free, open human family concerned with each other's welfare, sharing those life-giving resources which God and the Earth provides them, seeking no victories that require the pain and humiliation of others. They need no losers to prove their value to themselves, or to their neighbors, or to God. They seek only that gentle victory over terror or despair that they have always sought. They claim salvation in the reconciliation of the alienated, hurting and fallen humankind with the God who loves them, through the death and resurrection of Jesus Christ.

Consider the sinking of the freighter *Herald of Free Enterprise* on March 6, 1987. Those who recently risked their lives in the icy waters of the North Sea to rescue whomever they could aboard the capsized ferry made no distinction about who was worth saving and who wasn't. And yet every person rescued had, at least, the opportunity to examine his or her own actions as compared with those who rescued them. They were, in a sense, judged by their own rescue. They had the opportunity to ask themselves why they, of all people, were rescued. And if they were honest with themselves, they realized that they were rescued because their rescuers loved them simply because they were a part of the universal human family, a part of the world God loves so much. To rescue them, their rescuers had to put aside the fear of death, to act as if they themselves had been saved from the fear of death, a salvation that made this effort sacrificial, non-judgmental act of love a possibility for them.

From a sermon preached at Christ Church,
Cambridge, MA, March 15, 1987.

In the meantime, in expectation of the end, there is much to be done. Any household not ordered by force is ordered by politics, and the Christian lifestyle in a time such as this is intensely political. Our goals are simple enough, if not easy. We seek a radical redistribution of wealth, not just in our country but also in the world. We seek a society that is less centralized and made up of smaller economic, political, and institutional units. We want to see a less grandiose technology put to work for human beings in such a way to enhance rather than to dominate their lives while leaving the cosmic environment intact. We work for a federal economic policy of no growth where a high percentage of jobs are in the material and social maintenance of community life.

Obviously, we would like to see a number of things change, but as Christians we are not fools enough to think that our efforts to bring about these changes will be very effective in today's political climate. For us, politics is a kind of witness to our vision of reality, and it is important to make that witness again and again until Darwinist economics has finally discredited itself to the extent that a majority of people is seriously seeking an alternative. We are not in politics to succeed or to win; we are there to make available to all a vision of how Christians would have humans live together on this planet.[5]

5. As Christians began to suspect that the Second Coming of Christ might be delayed, they began to pay more and more heed for the morrow. The orderly transfer of property from generation to generation became more and more a concern. People worried about their heirs, about making the future "secure." The urge to accumulate was associated with the need to survive, and

A witness of political activism is, of course, not our only witness. There is the matter of how we live our lives together generally. To the extent that survival is not the primary motivating factor in our lives, we are not in competition with one another. But we must face the fact that survival is a large motivating factor and we are in competition with one another more than we realize. For the Christian, one must approach an ascetic lifestyle. The word "ascetic" derives from the Greek word for "ladder." *Ascesis* simply means, "climbing." Asceticism, then, is the classical term for spiritual growth. It is ancient wisdom that such growth is not accomplished by the accumulation of things, since human beings are inclined to put a kind of trust, almost a magical trust in things, and things have an extraordinary tendency to betray those who trust them. To this old wisdom, shared by many religions, Christianity has added a dimension of love. To use no more of creation than we need is a part of loving our neighbor. It is the most profound kind of sharing, because it is not sharing our surplus with someone else, it is sharing God's world with everyone else. It makes a statement about whose world this is.

Again, our purpose for living this way is to witness, to make precise theological statements about the nature of reality. We are not here to be in competition with our neighbor for survival. We are here to love God, and to love our neighbor as ourselves. We are also here to respect and care for the whole of creation, which God intends to be our home.

It is not until we have come to realize that we are not in this world to compete with our neighbor for survival that we can truly celebrate or give thanks for anything. Social Darwinists believe that they deserve whatever it is they get as long as it is good; and, consequently, they are not overcome with a sense of gratitude. But when we come to realize that we are not struggling against one

---

survival began to exert its imperialism over human consciousness. In all truth, the fear of death again became the shaping force of history, as hope for the immediate Second Coming waned. Soon, only the Saints sold their possessions and goods and distributed them to all, and "sainthood" was defined as a special vocation, and not the vocation of every Christian. Snow and Furnish, *Proclamation*, 17–18.

another to survive, that death is not the center of our lives since death has no ultimate dominion over our lives, we discover that we are possessed by a curious kind of freedom. It is, first of all, a freedom from illusion. We begin to get things straight, and that is something to celebrate and be thankful for, because we get things straight together. It is also a far greater freedom from fear than we have experienced before. Fear ceases to be the habitual climate of our decisions, and we can celebrate and give thanks to God for it. And we are freer to love in the felt knowledge that God loves us through Jesus Christ. We become essentially celebrative and thankful people.

We need to discover our common humanity, to learn from nature instead of insisting on force to create stalemates. How the Earth ignores us. How inevitably life breaks out of death. How the great wound of winter insists on healing itself. How the grey trees replenish themselves so urgently with green. Must our insane agony take place against this inexorable health? Can't we let go? Can't we let ourselves be reborn? Can't we give in to our baptism? The wind blows now, not the chill cutting wind of death, but the new, fresh, warming, bracing wind of spring, of Easter, of renewal and rebirth.

Right now inter-continental ballistic missiles pre-programmed toward each other's major cities make a strong case that force is a luxury we can no longer afford in the ordering of society. Love takes time.

From a sermon preached at Christ Church,
Cambridge, MA, April 13, 1969.

When, at the baptism of Jesus, God spoke and said, This is my beloved son with whom I am well pleased, God was addressing humanity. God was saying, If you want to know who I am, if you want to know what reality is, if you want to understand what I have created and why, and why I have created you, look very closely at the piece of history this baptism begins. This is the most complete answer you are ever going to get to these questions.

Look closely at this Jewish peasant standing in this dirty little creek. Keep your eyes on this man, listen to what he says, [and] watch how he deals with the people around him and the creation within which he moves. See how he addresses the sick, the crippled, the blind, and the deaf. See how he relates to outcasts and sinners. Listen to what he has to say to his enemies, to his persecutors, to the religious and secular authorities. See how he uses his time; what is important to him and unimportant to him. Watch him at weddings and funerals. See how he loves and cares about children. Pay attention to how he treats women and how quickly they understand who he is.

Consider his attitudes toward the use of force and violence. Notice his courage when he is afraid. Notice that there are things that make him angry, and pay attention to what they are. Notice how at home he is in the world, how he acts as if he has a right to be here, how he enjoys being here.

Appreciate his generosity of spirit, his hospitality, how he likes to feed and welcome anyone who comes along. And pay attention to how he dies, how his fear of pain and death do not stop his expression of love and concern for his friends and family. How alert he is to the pain of his neighbor in his own pain. How he meets death itself as a completion and perfection of his life, not as bad luck or a dirty trick.

But above all, continue to pay attention to when he dies. Watch as he is taken down from the cross and washed and wrapped in grave cloths by the women and put in a tomb, and notice a bit later that the tomb is empty. And notice how much this person, my beloved child, is like you.

> From a sermon preached at Christ Church,
> Cambridge, MA, December 29, 1991.
> In Snow, *A Vocation to Risk*, 29–30.

Afterword

Several months ago the Pew Research Center for Religion and Public Life released their findings from their most recent study (2007–2014) in a document entitled "America's Changing Religious Landscape." These researchers found that the identifiable Christian population had declined 7.8 percent over the last seven years, while those identifying with atheist, agnostic, and the unaffiliated rose by 6.1 percent.[1] *Christianity Today's* Ed Stetzer, commented, "facts are our friends and math is math," and he attributed the decline to the fact that not being religious is "more culturally savvy."[2] He went on to attribute the drift to those on the margins for whom religious affiliation no longer held a social importance that it once had. Stetzer has a point; not being religious is culturally more acceptable.

Thinking about this caused me to recall the millennial anniversary of the Russian Orthodox Church (1988). I remember my assistant preaching about this event. She said something to the effect that if you ask any orthodox priest the question of just how survival has been accomplished after decades / centuries

1. "America's Changing Religious Landscape," *Pew Research Center* (May 12, 2015), http://www.pewforum.org/2015/05/12/americas-changing-religious-landscape/.

2. Ed Stetzer, "Nominals to Nones: 3 Key Takeaways from Pew's Religious Landscape Survey," *Christianity Today* (May 12, 2015), http://www.christianitytoday.com/edstetzer/2015/may/nominals-to-nones-3-key-takeaways-from-pews-religious-lands.html.

of persecution, wars, opposition from governments, etc., his response will be, "We worship; success, numbers do not matter." At coffee hour she divided us into groups of eight and gave us the task of creating our own creed. Some broke out into laughter, others went about the task with the seriousness of a council; at report time each group admitted that they could only agree with a first sentence, "I believe in God."

Toward the end of his life, John Snow remarked to me that throughout his ministry he would lecture congregations about Social Darwinist reductionism. He said that those who listened to him became excited when he introduced the concept of Social Darwinism, saying in essence, "You're right, that is exactly how the world works!" Yet by the time he began talking about the rescue of people from quantifying and measuring each other and replacing that with love and forgiveness, they became "bored stiff" and called him "an 'idealist' with his Christian concerns."

Snow devoted his life to reorienting people to a Christian perspective on life's meaning, but to do so those in his audience would have to confront subjects that people avoid: the truth of Resurrection and the reality of death. One suspects that the former is more than just problematic; we are afraid it is not true. We ignore the latter.

Reflecting on my own ministry, many seem content to have the knowledge that their minister is religious. "I don't know what I believe," one parishioner said to me, "all that matters is if you'll be there for me if I need you." I replied, "That is a good place to start." Most people have limited time for religion, because, from their perspective, it seems not to apply to the way the world works. We are schooled in and focused on making a living, perfecting our trade, climbing up the proverbial ladder of life in order to make life as secure as possible for ourselves and our families and ensuring that our children have a better chance at the future than has been our lot. That is our focus. Such goals are laudable but they leave little time for serious reflection about life's or the church's real purpose; hence my question in my initial interview with John Snow.

First-hand experience with the application of our faith is rare. Serious theological reflection is even more difficult. Group behavior in church is regulated by cultural norms. Outside the church we revert to being the fittest for survival, even if it is at the expense of others. While we don't beat each other up physically, social competition is rigorous. While we know we shouldn't label each other by race or by religion, red-lined real-estate boundaries separate communities of different ethnic or racial compositions. We know shouldn't belittle each other vocationally, but lines exist between trades and professions on levels of education, sophistication, and income. It is the way the world works. A few discover, as Joseph Campbell has observed, that once they get to the top of their ladder, they find that it is propped against the "wrong wall."

I believe that the attractiveness of Social Darwinism is that it produces a quick solution to life's purpose. Our national and individual notions of exceptionalism presuppose the inexhaustibility of our resources as well as personal indemnity from death. We shall be saved from our wastefulness as well as from death by the kindly and cornucopian nature of our creator. Neither assumption makes sense but comes our way because "it is the way the world works." Competition for resources or for place exists because we do not want someone else to have these resources or to be ahead of us.

I hold to the broader notion that religion helps us "to get life right," as I used to say from my own pulpit. That the word "religion" derives its meaning from the Latin root *ligio* from which we get our word *ligament*, meaning *bound together*. Thus we are accountable to each other as well as to the divine.

Since the Gospels are compendiums of remembered tales converging from many sources, we must remember the truth of these stories and disregard them as literal fact. The breaking down of death-dealing boundaries of social exclusion, isolation, ignorance illness, judgment, and fear is what the Good News is all about. It refers us to a love present and manifest in Jesus that is stronger than death. It is always found in truth, acceptance, forgiveness, love, and hope. This is the mystery of life and a God who made it visible in Jesus.

I believe that Jesus did not know of or anticipate resurrection; he did not know of or believe in his own divinity . . . he lived resurrection without forethought. He fed, empowered, healed, and affirmed humankind in ways that produced hope, love, and new life. Scripture documents what Jesus did because what happened came from a surprising source, a powerless person who told stories and did acts to empower new life in a very oppressed and subjugated people—his peers.

I came across a paper written by sociologist Charles Lemert, some time after my retirement from parish ministry, which reinforces my view. Dr. Lemert writes:

> Religion may be the most important source of realism. Religion, thus, and most elementally, is the form of social life in which people together, whatever their differences, understand themselves as doubly finite. As individuals, we cannot transcend the social relations that form us. As members with *all* others, we cannot escape the limitations of our humanity . . . Utopias are different from heavens, they being the liberal dreams of human aspiration. Heaven, by contrast, is the metaphoric expression of the human ideal that, being commonly limited, we are bound to all others, even those of a different social kind. Human justice will come, perhaps when we recognize that we, among all others, have no greater or lesser need for recognition or for our daily bread.[3]

The last letter I received from John (February 8, 2006) concluded with a short reflection on his life. He lamented the fact that people dismissed notions of religion. He said in essence:

> I've come on to some really difficult problems in my life and I've experienced serious doubt. While we seem to be hurtling toward the abyss, I've found that if I have something big or troublesome in front of me, if you just dive right into it, you're always bound to find light. Pierre

3. Lemert, "The Might Have Been and Could Be of Religion in Social Theory," 261.

Teilhard de Chardin calls it a "common consciousness" with God. It gives me comfort.

John also said: "Resurrection is not survival. It makes survival unnecessary."

Selected Bibliography

Bateson, Gregory. *Steps to an Ecology of the Mind*. Chicago, IL: University of Chicago Press, 1972.

Berry, Wendell. "Faustian Economics." *Harpers Magazine* (May 2008): 35–42. http://harpers.org/archive/2008/05/faustian-economics/.

Bion, Wilfred R. *Experiences in Groups*. New York: Routledge, 1968.

Carneiro, Robert J. ed. *Herbert Spencer: The Evolution of Society*. Chicago: University of Chicago Press, 1967.

de Chardin, Pierre Teilhard. *The Phenomenon of Man*. New York: Harper and Brothers, 1959.

Denby, David. "Winners and Losers." *The New Yorker* (December 2, 2013): 66–68.

"The Donald S. Frederickson Papers: The Controversy over the Regulation of Recombinant DNA Research, 1975–1981." *Profiles in Science of the National Library of Medicine*. http://www.profiles.nlm.nih.gov/ps/retrieve/Narrative/FF/p-nid/74.

Elbow, Peter. *Writing Without Teachers*. New York: Oxford University Press, 1973.

Erlich, H. Samuel. "Dependency, Autonomy and the Politics of Survival." In *Organizational and Social Dynamics*, vol. 4, 285–297. London: Karnac, 2004.

Galeano, Eduardo. *Mirrors: Stories of Almost Everyone*. New York: Nation, 2009.

Hawkins, Mike. *Social Darwinism in European and American Thought, 1860–1945*. New York: Cambridge University Press, 1997.

Hofstadter, Richard. *Social Darwinism in American Thought*. Boston: Beacon, 1992.

John Locke: An Essay Concerning Human Understanding. Edited by Gary Fuller, Robert Stecker, and John P. Wright. New York: Routledge, 2000.

Kets de Vries, F. R. Manfred. *The Neurotic Organization: Counterproductive Styles of Management*. San Francisco, CA: Jossey-Bass, 1984.

Kung, Hans. *On Being a Christian*. New York: Doubleday, 1966.

Lemert, Charles C. "The Might Have Been and Could Be of Religion in Social Theory." *Social Sciences Division II Faculty Publications*, Paper 8 (2002): 240–263. http://wesscholar.wesleyan.edu/cgi/viewcontent.cgi?article=1007&context=div2facpubs.

Lorenz, Konrad. "1973 Nobel Prize Biographical Statement." In *Nobel Lectures in Physiology or Medicine 1971–1980*. Edited by Jan Lindsten. Singapore: World Scientific Publishing Company, 1992, www.nobelprize.org/nobel_prizes/medicine/laureates/1973/lorenz-bio.html.

Lodge, George C. *The New American Ideology*. New York: Alfred A. Knopf, 1974.

Maccoby, Michael. *The Gamesman: The New Corporate Leaders*. New York: Simon and Schuster, 1976.

Malcom, Janet. *The Impossible Profession*. New York: Vintage, 1980.

Miller, David. *Political Philosophy: A Very Short Introduction*. New York: Oxford University Press, 2003.

Percy, Walker. "A Theory of Language." In Percy Walker, *The Message in the Bottle*, 298–329. New York: Farrar, Straus and Giroux, 1975.

Peel, J.D.Y., ed. *Herbert Spencer on Social Evolution*. Chicago: University of Chicago Press, 1972

Schon, Donald A. *The Reflective Practitioner: How Professionals Think in Action*. New York: Basic Books, 1984

Snow, John H. *A Vocation to Risk: Notes on Ministry in a Profane World*. Boston, MA: Cowley, 1992.

———. "Midlife Crises and Theological Reconstruction." *Studies in Formative Spirituality* 11:1 (1990): 7–21.

———. *Mortal Fear: Meditations on Death and AIDS*. Cambridge, MA: Cowley, 1987.

———. *On Pilgrimage: Marriage in the '70s*. New York: Seabury, 1971.

———. "The Conflict Between Social Darwinism and the Power of Purpose: A Personal Reflection." Unpublished manuscript, n.d.

Snow, John H. and Victor P. Furnish. *Proclamation: Aids for Interpreting the Lessons of the Church Year*, Series A—Easter. Philadelphia: Fortress, 1975.

———. *The Gospel in a Broken World*. Philadelphia: Pilgrim, 1972.

———. *The Impossible Vocation: Ministry in the Meantime*. Cambridge, MA: Cowley, 1988.

Snow, John H. with Frederick Stecker. "American Social Darwinism Makes Us Less Civilized." *Clio's Psyche*. 21:3 (2014): 288–291

Soelle, Dorothee. *Choosing Life*. Philadelphia: Fortress, 1981.

Stecker, Frederick. *The Podium, the Pulpit, and the Republicans: How Presidential Candidates Use Religious Language in American Political Debate*. Santa Barbara, CA: Praeger, 2011.

Stone, Leo. *Transference and its Context*. New York: Jason Aronson, 1977.

Swimme, Brian. *The New Natural Selection*. Teilhard Studies No. 10. Chambersberg, PA: Anima, 1983.

Terkel, Studs. *My American Century*. New York: The New Press, 1997.

Selected Bibliography

Updike, John. "When Everyone was Pregnant." In John Updike, *Museums and Women, and Other Stories*, 91–97. New York: Alfred A. Knopf, 1972.

Wolson, Peter. "The Existential Dimension of Psychoanalysis (EDP): Psychic Survival and the Fear of Psychic Death (Nonbeing)." *Psychoanalytic Review* 92 (2005): 675–699.